THE LAW

OF

MENTAL MEDICINE

THE CORRELATION OF THE FACTS OF PSYCHOLOGY AND HISTOLOGY IN THEIR RELATION TO MENTAL THERAPEUTICS

BY

THOMSON JAY HUDSON, Ph.D., LL.D.

AUTHOR OF "THE LAW OF PSYCHIC PHENOMENA,"
"THE DIVINE PEDIGREE OF MAN," ETC.

SECOND EDITION

CHICAGO
A. C. McCLURG & CO.
1903

C000100236

COPYRIGHT

B⟨ A. C. McClurg & Co.

A.D. 1903

Published May 23, 1903

Second Edition, June 15, 1903

UNIVERSITY PRESS · JOHN WILSON
AND SON CAMBRIDGE, U. S. A

**Kessinger Publishing's Rare Reprints
Thousands of Scarce and Hard-to-Find Books!**

We kindly invite you to view our extensive catalog list at:
http://www.kessinger.net

BY DR. HUDSON.

◆

THE LAW OF PSYCHIC PHENOMENA.
12mo $1.50

A SCIENTIFIC DEMONSTRATION OF THE
FUTURE LIFE. 12mo 1.50

THE DIVINE PEDIGREE OF MAN. 12mo. 1.50

THE LAW OF MENTAL MEDICINE. 12mo.
1.20 *net*

◆

A. C McCLURG & CO.
CHICAGO.

TO

THE HONORABLE

DON M. DICKINSON

IN GRATEFUL ACKNOWLEDGMENT OF A FRIENDSHIP

THAT, FOR A PERIOD OF TIME EXCEEDING

THE AVERAGE LIFE OF MAN,

HAS KNOWN NO VARIABLENESS OR SHADOW OF TURNING,

𝕿𝖍𝖎𝖘 𝕭𝖔𝖔𝖐

IS AFFECTIONATELY INSCRIBED

PREFACE

THE object of this book is, primarily, to assist in placing mental therapeutics on a firmly scientific basis, and incidentally to place within the reach of the humblest intellect the most effective methods of healing the sick by mental processes.

Part I. contains nothing new to the scientific world, except, perhaps, the method of treatment. It pertains solely to the psychological principles of mental medicine. These were outlined in my first work, entitled "The Law of Psychic Phenomena," ten years ago, and they are now taught in every reputable school of suggestive therapeutics. The reader will find, however, that the subject is by no means exhausted, and that the law of suggestion is the most important factor in man's mental make-up.

In Part II. the fact is for the first time recognized that no hypothesis can possibly embrace a complete science of mental therapeutics that fails to take cognizance of those facts of physiology and histology which pertain to the subject-matter. Necessarily, the subjective mind, when it exercises its powers over the body, in health and disease, operates through instrumentalities; that is to say, there must exist a physical mechanism through which the mind operates, and that mechanism must necessarily be adapted to its uses. Moreover, we might reasonably expect that the mechanism, when found, would be so obviously adapted to therapeutic uses as to leave no doubt in the mind of the investigator. Accordingly we find in man a physical structure so obviously adapted to the uses of mental healing that it leaves one in doubt whether or not all therapeutic agencies, in their ultimate analysis, may not be classed as mental. Be that as it may, it is obvious that a correlation of the facts of psychology and histology must lead to some very valuable discoveries, not alone in the field of mental therapeutics, but in all branches of inquiry where the control of the body by the mind is a factor. A few of these discoveries are outlined in the following pages. Without stopping to enumerate them in detail, I think I am justified in claiming to have thrown much light upon some very obscure problems; for instance, the method of healing which in ancient times was known as "the laying on of hands," and in modern times has been designated as " animal magnetism," " mesmerism," etc I have also incidentally touched upon the problem of natural sleep, and I have tentatively suggested a solution of the world-old problem, What are the physical changes that produce the phenomenon of unconsciousness during natural sleep? If my hypothesis is correct on this question, it simplifies the whole subject-matter, and throws a flood of light upon hypnotism and all other forms of artificial sleep.

In pursuing my investigations of the physical sciences bearing upon the question of mental healing, I have been careful to confine myself to authorities which are recognized by the modern scientists of the medical profession; and I here take occasion to acknowledge my indebtedness, fearing that in the hurry of writing I may have failed to give credit where credit is due. The principal works consulted are the following: Gray's Anatomy; Landois and Stirling's Text-book of Human Physiology; Bohm-Davidoff's Text-book of Histology; Green's Pathology and Morbid Anatomy; Dunham's Histology, Normal and Morbid; Stephens's Pluricellular Man; Hilton's Lectures on Rest and Pain; Halleck's Education of the Central Nervous System; Robinson's The Abdominal Brain; Romanes' Mental Evolution in Animals; Romanes' Animal Intelligence; Avebury's (Sir John Lubbock) Ants, Bees, and Wasps; Binet's The Psychic Life of Micro-organisms; Haeckel's The Evolution of Man; Ochorowicz's Mental Suggestion.

T. J. H.

DETROIT, MICH., May 1, 1903.

CONTENTS

Part One

THE PSYCHOLOGICAL PRINCIPLES INVOLVED IN MENTAL HEALING

CHAPTER I

INTRODUCTORY

PAGE

Ancient Superstitions. — All Diseases referred to Bad Spirits. — All Healing of Disease credited to Good Spirits. — Innumerable Theories of Causation prevalent among Primitive Peoples. — Many of them still survive in Modified Forms; some of the most grotesque being extremely popular in the midst of the Highest Civilization. — All Systems, Ancient and Modern, have been successful in healing the Sick. — This Fact alone challenges the Attention of Science. — It indicates the Existence of a Law pertaining generically to all Systems. — No Logical Connection between Theories of Causation and the Results produced; otherwise all Systems, from Fetichism to the most Modern Modification of that System, would be able to "demonstrate" their Theories. — The Logic of Primitive Minds the same in all the Ages. — The Question of Mental Healing is primarily a psychological one; hence the Necessity of studying the Fundamental Principles of Psychology as a Basis of a Correct Theory of Causation. — Recent Discovery of a Primary Intelligence below the Threshold of Normal Consciousness enables us to study the Subject inductively. — The Facts of Physiology and Histology reveal the Rationale of Mental Healing. — It is unnecessary to antagonize Established Systems of Material Therapeutics. — We are indebted to Doctors of Medicine for much of the Knowledge which enables us to formulate a Rational Theory. — The Correlation of all the Facts of Psychology and Physiology is

CHAPTER II

FIRST PRINCIPLES

CHAPTER III

THE VARIOUS SYSTEMS OF MENTAL HEALING

CHAPTER IV

THE DUPLEX MENTAL ORGANISM

CHAPTER V

THE LAW OF SUGGESTION (HISTORICAL)

CHAPTER VI

SUGGESTION IN LOWER ANIMAL LIFE

CHAPTER VII

SUGGESTIONS ADVERSE TO HEALTH

CHAPTER VIII

" PURITANICAL " DIET AND MEDICINE

CHAPTER IX

AUTO-SUGGESTION

Part Two

THE CORRELATION OF THE FACTS OF PSYCHOLOGY AND PHYSIOLOGY IN CONNECTION WITH MENTAL HEALING

CHAPTER I

INTRODUCTORY

The Facts of Psychology and Physiology to be Correlated. — All Organic Tissue composed of Intelligent Microscopic Cells. — Disease of the Body is Disease of the Cells of the Body. — The Cells amenable to Control by the Subjective Mind. — The Fluidic

CHAPTER II

THE PHYSICAL MECHANISM THROUGH WHICH MENTAL HEALING
IS EFFECTED

CHAPTER III

THE PHYSICAL MECHANISM THROUGH WHICH MENTAL HEALING
IS EFFECTED (*Continued*)

CHAPTER IV

THE MECHANISM OF INHIBITION

CHAPTER V

INHIBITION AND SLEEP, NATURAL AND INDUCED

CHAPTER VI

ANIMAL MAGNETISM, HYPNOTISM, AND LAYING ON OF HANDS

CHAPTER VII

THOUGHT-TRANSFERENCE BY ANTS AND BEES BY MEANS OF PHYSICAL CONTACT

CHAPTER VIII

THOUGHT-TRANSFERENCE BY MAN UNDER CONDITIONS OF PHYSICAL CONTACT

CHAPTER IX

CONCLUSIONS — THEORETICAL AND PRACTICAL

Part One

THE PSYCHOLOGICAL PRINCIPLES INVOLVED IN MENTAL HEALING

THE LAW OF MENTAL MEDICINE

———◆———

Part One

THE PSYCHOLOGICAL PRINCIPLES INVOLVED IN MENTAL HEALING

————

CHAPTER I

INTRODUCTORY

Ancient Superstitions. — All Diseases referred to Bad Spirits. — All Healing of Disease credited to Good Spirits. — Innumerable Theories of Causation prevalent among Primitive Peoples. — Many of them still survive in Modified Forms; some of the most grotesque being extremely popular in the midst of the Highest Civilization. — All Systems, Ancient and Modern, have been successful in healing the Sick. — This Fact alone challenges the Attention of Science. — It indicates the Existence of a Law pertaining generically to all Systems. — No Logical Connection between Theories of Causation and the Results produced; otherwise all Systems, from Fetichism to the most Modern Modification of that System, would be able to "demonstrate" their Theories. — The Logic of Primitive Minds the same in all the Ages. — The Question of Mental Healing is primarily a psychological one; hence the Necessity of studying the Fundamental Principles of Psychology as a Basis of a Correct Theory of Causation. — Recent Discovery of a Primary Intelligence below the Threshold of Normal Consciousness enables us to study the Subject inductively. — The Facts of Physiology and Histology reveal the Rationale of Mental Healing. — It is unnecessary to antagonize Established Systems of Material Therapeutics. — We are indebted to Doctors of Medicine for much of the Knowledge which enables us to formulate a Rational Theory. — The Correlation of all the Facts of Psychology and Physiology are necessary for placing Mental Therapeutics on a Scientific Basis. — Many Medical Men employ the Methods of Suggestive Therapeutics in their Daily Practice. — The Discovery of the Law of Suggestion by a Number of the Medical Profession was the first Great Step in the Direction of a True Explication of Mental Therapeutics. — The next Great Step was its Generalization under the Law of the Duality of Mind. — The Correlation of all the Facts of Mental and Physical Science is therefore essential.

HISTORY informs us that in all the ages man has recognized the existence of an intelligent Power capable of creating diseases in the human body, and of healing them independently of material remedies or appliances. This Power, being invisible and intangible, was very naturally referred to mental or spiritual agencies, good or bad, beneficent or malevolent, as the symptoms in each particular case seemed to indicate. In the early days " spirits of health " and " goblins damned " seem to have peopled the circumambient air in vast numbers and in about equal proportions. One host revisited " the glimpses of the moon" with intents decidedly wicked; the other with those that were purely charitable. One brought blasts from hell: the other breathed airs from heaven. One sent forth plague and pestilence; the other shed healing from its wings. For untold ages these invisible agencies, good and bad, seem to have been practically the only ones held responsible for the existence of disease, or credited with the power of healing the sick.

Naturally, the greatest efforts of men so beset by the conflicting forces surrounding them were employed in devising ways and means for thwarting the efforts of the evil spirits and for conciliating those that were good. Hence the innumerable recipes for those purposes which history informs us were in common use among our remote ancestors. A volume would be required even to catalogue the various devices and formulas for invoking the aid of the health-purveying inhabitants of the spirit world, to say nothing of the " prophylactical receipts of wholesome caution " against evil spirits in general and witches in particular. Such a volume, compiled from all available sources, would be of incalculable value to science; for it would show that not only our ancestors — savage, semi-civilized, and civilized — were filled with such superstitions, but that all primitive peoples have had, and still have, the same generic ideas, and that they practise generically the same methods of healing the sick. What is of still greater importance, it would show that all the facts of spiritual or mental healing among primitive peoples of all the ages are easily correlated not only with each other, but with many of the methods now in vogue in the most highly civilized nations. That is to say, many of the modern theories of causation are mere survivals of ancient superstitions; and some of them differ from the latter only in the more accentuated and grotesque imbecility of the later theories of causation.

More important still is the fact that the records show that under all " systems," ancient and modern, many marvellous cures have been effected, some of them seemingly miraculous. This fact, to the inductive scientist. is pregnant with significance; for it is demonstrative that the whole subject-matter is under the dominion of some natural law. The scientist reasons thus: Here is a vast congeries of phenomena to be accounted for. They have been produced in every age and in every tribe and nation in the world, civilized and savage. Some of the phenomena, it is true, may be accounted for on the score of mal-observation: some may be attributed to fraud and legerdemain, and much to defective memory or intentional falsehood. But after due allowance is made for these and other minor sources of error, the great bulk of the phenomena remains to challenge the attention of the scientist. It is true that science in years gone by has not deigned to meddle with the subject, choosing to relegate all the alleged phenomena indiscriminately to the domain of superstition and imposture. During the last decade, however, it has become evident to the most skeptical that cures of disease are being effected, in the midst of the highest civilization, by means obviously identical with those employed in the darkest ages of superstition. That is to say, the results are identical: and it is axiomatic that, in any series of cognate phenomena, identical results presuppose identical or cognate causes. Hence it is that when, as in mental healing, uniform results are reported from widely separated localities, from all races and conditions of mankind during all the ages, ancient and modern, the true scientist knows that there must be a basis of truth underlying the whole subject, and that all the phenomena are referable to some one generic cause. Nor does the multiplicity of theories of causation held by the various tribes of men, or sects of mental healers, militate in the least against the student's convictions; for if he has acquired the most superficial acquaintance with the elementary principles of logic, he is aware that there is no necessary connection between theories of causation and the results produced by those who hold them. In other words, the fact of healing the sick by any method whatever does not demonstrate the correctness of the theory of causation which happens to be entertained by the healer in any given case.

This is a self-evident proposition; and to the average reader it will seem to be a work of supererogation to state it formally. But it must be remembered that there are vast numbers of mental healers, in this and other highly civilized countries, whose theories of causation are more fantastic, not to say idiotic, than those of any savage tribe of which history informs us, and that they firmly and fervently believe and proclaim that their theories are demonstrated to be true by the fact that they heal the sick. In fact, so insistent are they upon this point that they habitually employ the word " demonstrate," or some of its derivatives, as a synonym for the verb " to heal." Every act of healing, in other words, is a complete demonstration of the truth of the hypothesis which the healer happens to entertain.

It is, perhaps, superfluous to add that if this were true of one system of mental healing it would be true of all. Hence the North American Indian, whose theory of disease is that it is caused by the infernal machinations of evil spirits, and whose therapeutic agencies consist in frightening away said evil spirits by means of hideous noises and a diabolical "make up," has the same logical right to claim that successful healing by his system is demonstrative of the correctness of his theory of disease as well as of the scientific value of his methods of healing. What is true of the North American Indian's hypothesis is true of all theories of disease and all therapeutic agencies, in Christian or in heathen lands; for, as before remarked, the one salient fact that correlates all systems of mental medicine is that they all heal the sick.

It is this one fact that challenges the attention of science. It appeals to the anthropologist, because the beliefs of mankind, whether true or false, constitute an important branch of his curriculum of studies. It is of infinite interest and importance to the therapeutist, because it is demonstrative that in some way the state of the mind of the patient is an important factor in the diagnosis and treatment of disease. But its most direct and imperative appeal is to the psychologist; for it is primarily a purely psychological question, and upon the student of that science devolves the task of discovering the fundamental principles underlying the mental force behind the phenomena. When that is accomplished, it will be next in order to invoke the aid of physiology, and especially of microscopic anatomy, or histology, to the end that we may learn something of the machinery through which this potent energy performs its work.

It is obvious that if even the fundamentals of this knowledge can be successfully acquired, we may then know, proximately at least, something of the *modus operandi* by which the mind acts upon the body in health and in the cure of disease. It follows that such knowledge will enable us to direct the healing energy more intelligently, and presumably more effectively. Not that we can ever learn just how the mind performs its functions as a therapeutic agent. We do not even know how it causes the simplest movement of the limbs, although we may be conscious of imparting the primary mental stimulus necessary to produce that result in the voluntary muscles. Science has taught us something of the machinery through which the mind operates to produce consciously a voluntary movement of the body. We know by conscious experience that the mind is the motive power; and we have taken a few primary lessons in the art of directing and controlling that power and making it useful. But this is all that we really know of that conscious intelligence which, nevertheless, has elevated mankind from savagery to civilization.

How little man knows of his own mental powers and limitations is shown in the fact that it is only within the last decade that he has become aware of the existence. within himself and below the threshold of his normal consciousness, of a primary [1] intelligence that is at once endowed with wonderful powers and circumscribed by equally wonderful limitations. It is well within the bounds of truth to say that it is to this discovery that the world is indebted for all the knowledge that it possesses of the real

---

[1] Some authors denominate this intelligence "the *secondary* self," but the facts of organic evolution show conclusively that it is the *primary* intelligence of the organic world. See "The Divine Pedigree of Man."

science of mental therapeutics; for it is to this primary intelligence that science has traced the source of the mental power that heals; and it is to its limitations that is due all that is mysterious in its phenomenal manifestations, not only in the domain of mental therapeutics, but in all other classes of psychical phenomena.

In attempting an analysis of this wonderful subjective intelligence I shall confine myself to its aspects as a therapeutic agent, and not obtrude any theories or speculations as to its ultimate origin [1] or its final destiny.[2] I shall confine myself exclusively to the demonstrable facts of experimental psychology for my proofs of the existence of a subjective intelligence, to the well-authenticated experiences of mankind for proofs of its potency as a healing agent, and to the current standard literature of physiology and histology to show the rationale of the mental processes by which every fibre of the body is reached, and its conditions controlled. I do not expect to say the last word that can be said of the science of mental therapeutics; but my primary object will be accomplished if I can point out the lines of study and investigation which may lead to an intelligent solution of the problem of mental control over the body in health and disease. If in addition to that I can succeed in discovering the fundamental psychological law pertaining to the control of the healing power resident in every man's mental organism, and in pointing out the physical mechanism through which that power is exerted, I may hope to be able

[1] See "The Divine Pedigree of Man"
[2] See "A Scientific Demonstration of the Future Life."

to indicate the most effective methods of practising the healing art without the use of material remedies.

Before proceeding to the discussion of the main subject, however, I desire to say a word in regard to doctors of medicine.

I have no quarrel with the medical profession, nor can I join in the indiscriminate clamor against material remedies for the cure of disease. I cannot forget that doctors of medicine were the first to discover the fundamental facts which lie at the basis of the science of mental medicine. Thus, Dr. Hack Tuke's great work [1] contains a voluminous record of the observations of cases by medical men, of both ancient and modern times, demonstrating the control of the mind over the body in health and disease. Indeed the literature of medicine, within the memory of men now living, was full of illustrations of that important fact; and medical students were instructed by their professors in its practical application at the bedside. A cheerful, hopeful, and, above all, a confident demeanor was held to be only second in importance to the material remedies prescribed; and, to give the profession due credit, the effect of that instruction still survives, and is visibly manifested in the wise and preternaturally able expression of countenance which every physician knows so well how to assume when feeling the pulse, examining the tongue, and writing the prescription. The Law of Suggestion had not been formulated when such instructions became a part of the college curriculum, but its practical value was thus recognized by the

[1] The Influence of Mind upon the Body (Henry C. Lea's Son & Co., Philadelphia).

medical profession many generations before Braid or Liébault saw the light; and the medical doctor who first prescribed a placebo,[1] under the guise of a specific, and noted its wonderful curative powers, took the first great step in demonstrating the therapeutic value of a "larvated" (Pitzer) suggestion. It may be noted, in passing, that one of the most hopeful indications of advancement in medical science consists in the fact that the profession now very generally recognize the placebo as indicated when diagnosis fails. Manufacturing pharmacists consequently derive a large income from the sale of the ready-made placebo. That many fatal mistakes have been avoided by its employment, and many cures effected, goes without saying.

It will thus be seen that to the medical profession the world is indebted for two discoveries, — first, that the mind controls the bodily functions; second, that the mind can be controlled by suggestion. That physicians did not formulate the law, and builded better than they knew, does not detract from their merits as original discoverers. Columbus died in ignorance of the fact that he had discovered America.

Nor can I follow the extremists in holding that all material remedies, like the placebo, owe their efficacy wholly to suggestion. I recognize the fact — which the medical profession has taught us — that the human body is made up of an aggregation, or confederation, of cells; that each cell is an individual entity, a living creature, and that, as such, it performs all the functions of animal life, including those of nutrition, digestion, and excretion. Each

---

[1] Commonly called "bread pills."

cell, therefore, requires its appropriate food to enable it to perform its special functions. This food is, of course, supplied from the material taken into the stomach; and the blood-cells perform the double duty of conveying the food to each individual cell, and of removing the waste material excreted (metabolism). It follows that the useful food-material of all that is taken into the stomach, be it in ordinary food or in medicine, is carried to its appropriate groups of cells. That some medicines contain nutritive material adapted to the needs of special groups of cells cannot be seriously doubted. Nor can it be doubted that if the medical profession could know just what material is adapted to the necessities of each group of cells. medicine would assume the dignity of an inductive science. They have already laid the foundation for the study of medicine on those lines by their minute researches in the science of histology, or microscopic anatomy, which is the branch of biology that treats of the cell life and the structure of the tissues of organized bodies. They have also laid a broad foundation for the study of the true science of mental medicine, by revealing the machinery through which suggestion does its therapeutic work. It enables us not only to correlate all systems of mental healing, ancient and modern, but to harmonize the facts of suggestive therapeutics with the accepted principles of modern physiological science as laid down by the ablest medical authorities.

It must also be remembered to the credit of the medical profession that one of its members formulated the Law of Suggestion, and thus laid the foundation of the science of mental healing. It is true

that it was formulated with special reference to hypnotism; but at that time hypnotism was the only
phase of psychic phenomena under scientific discussion.   Later on, a broader generalization became
necessary in connection with the theory of the dual
mind, and the law was then found to pertain exclusively to the subjective mind, and to dominate that
mysterious mental force under all its states and conditions.[1]   Nevertheless, the discovery of the Law of
Suggestion in its relations to hypnotism was the
first great step in the direction of a true explication,
not only of mental therapeutics. but of all psychic
phenomena.

It is true that the attitude of the medical profession toward all forms and theories of mental therapeutics has always been one of extreme conservatism.
often savoring of unreasoning prejudice; but on the
whole its influence has been salutary.   If its denun-
ciations have been bitter, it was because they have
been directed chiefly against charlatanism and unscientific theories of causation; but, as I shall attempt to show, its inductions and discoveries have
furnished the basis of a scientific system of mental
therapeutics.

It will now be seen that I am not about to wage
a warfare against the medical profession, nor upon
drugs and medicines. nor upon any of the so-called
" systems " of mental therapeutics, much less upon
the well-ascertained facts of physiological science.   It
is a truism of science that, in the investigation of any
subject. no fact can safely be ignored that pertains,
directly or indirectly, to the subject-matter; for no

---

[1] See " The Law of Psychic Phenomena "

fact in nature is inconsistent with any other fact. If, therefore, it is true that the mind controls the bodily functions in health and disease, the facts of physiological science will at least harmonize with the proposition, and perchance reveal approximately something of the methods and machinery by which this control is effected. In other words, psychology and physiology necessarily touch upon each other somewhere; and it is the object of this book to suggest tentatively a line of study by which the facts of both sciences, so far as they relate to mental therapeutics, may be correlated and reduced to something like scientific coherency. An exhaustive treatise is, of course, impossible within the limits prescribed; but if I can induce abler men to test the value of my suggestions, I am not without hope that a truly scientific system of psycho-therapeutics may eventually be evolved which will harmonize all the facts of human experience that pertain to the subject-matter.

I shall first treat of the psychological aspects of the question; secondly, of the psycho-physiological; and, thirdly, of the methods of practice which suggest themselves in view of all the facts developed.

CHAPTER II

FIRST PRINCIPLES

Mental Healing is not a Religion. — The Example of Jesus is conclusive on that Point — Nothing Supernatural in Mental Medicine. — The Power that Heals resides within the Patient. — This was the Doctrine taught by Jesus and epitomized in the Words " Thy Faith hath made Thee whole." — The Word " Faith," as he employed it, means not only "Belief" or "Confidence." but includes all the Spiritual Energies of the Human Soul. — It is not only prerequisite to Success in Mental Healing, but is a Dynamic Energy, besides. — Modern Science has succeeded only in demonstrating the Scientific Accuracy of the Master's Knowledge of Mental Therapeutics. — The Whole Art of Mental Healing consists in knowing how to induce the Condition of Faith in the Patient. — The Fundamental Psychological Principles involved. — Suggestion a Universal Law of the Subjective Mind — Limitations of Subjective Powers of Reasoning. — False and True Suggestions. — Potency of Auto-Suggestions. — Moral Principles constitute Auto-Suggestions — Resistance to False Suggestions. — Effectiveness of Suggestion not dependent upon the Hypnotic Condition — Passivity of the Mind the Equivalent of Hypnosis for Therapeutic Purposes. — Suggestions based upon Scientific Truth are most effective — The Third Fundamental Psychological Principle.

BEFORE attempting to state what mental healing is, it may be well to have a clear understanding of what it is not. First, then, it is not a religion. There is no more religion in healing the sick by mental processes than there is in healing them by pills or clysters Many good people think otherwise, and cite the example of the Master. But there is no evidence that he regarded the act of healing as a religious rite, except in so far as all benevolent acts belong to that scheme of universal altruism which was the essence of his religion. But he exacted no precedent conditions of religious belief from the beneficiaries of his power; he prescribed for them no acts of religious worship, nor did he himself perform any in connection with the exercise of his healing power. The only thing that savored of religion, therefore, was in that which he refrained from doing, namely: he accepted no fees for his services, nor did he charge his apostles for " lessons."

Secondly, there is nothing supernatural or supermundane in the methods or agencies employed in healing the sick by mental processes; and thirdly, no power or agency, mundane or supermundane, extraneous to the patient himself, has any part or lot in the process of mental healing. For proof of these two propositions we may again refer to the authority of the Master. And this brings us to the immediate consideration of the question what mental healing is.

Those who are acquainted with the history and teachings of Jesus of Nazareth, as set forth in the New Testament, will recall the facts that he never claimed any credit for healing the sick; nor did he arrogate to himself the possession of any personal power to heal disease; much less did he ascribe the power to any other agency, human or divine, extraneous to the patient himself. In truth, the reticence of Jesus in regard to his attributes and powers was one of his most marked characteristics. But more remarkable still was the fact that what he did say was always pregnant with veritable scientific signifi-

2

cance. No better illustration of this can be imagined than his constantly reiterated statement with regard to the real source of the healing power manifested in his patients. The words " Thy faith hath made thee whole " constitute a scientifically exact statement of the fundamental fact of mental therapeutics. Their obvious meaning is, first. that the power which effects the healing is resident within the patient, and not in any extraneous force or agency. This is the primary meaning of the phrase, and no amount of sophistry can weaken its force or significance. Secondly, it means that this force or energy resident within the patient consists of, or is due to, a certain definite mental condition or attitude of mind with reference to the work to be done. It may be here remarked that the English word " faith " very inadequately describes the energy or force in question, as Jesus apparently understood it. That is to say, no definition of the word is found in any dictionary that conveys the slightest notion of that dynamic energy which enabled the leper to throw off his disease instantaneously, or the lame man to take up his bed and walk. Every dictionary definition embraces the implication of some form or degree of *belief* as its determinative feature. But the faith which Jesus proclaimed as the one prepotent agency in the healing of disease, — the faith which sustained Peter in his walk upon the water until he momentarily lost it, the dynamic potentialities of which could only be adequately prefigured as being equal to the removal of mountains, — such a faith is necessarily far more than the word " belief " or " confidence " would imply. It includes both, as modern experiments amply demonstrate; but it must also include all the spiritual energies of the human soul. To say the least, it must be the mental condition precedent to enable the soul to exercise any of its powers.

Be that as it may, it is sufficient for present purposes to know that faith is the essential mental condition prerequisite to success in healing the sick by any process of mental healing; and when Jesus of Nazareth proclaimed that pregnant fact, he anticipated the inductions of modern science by nineteen hundred years. How he came into possession of such an exact knowledge of the fundamental law of mental healing, is not a pertinent subject of discussion in this connection. It is sufficient to note the fact that he possessed that knowledge. Science is concerned only with the question of verification. That it has been amply verified by scientific experimentation within the last quarter of a century is a matter of common knowledge among students of experimental psychology. The nature of the experiments and their evidential value will be shown hereinafter. In the meantime we must assume provisionally that a certain definite attitude of mind on the part of the patient is essential to success in mental healing, and that that attitude of mind is best defined by the word "faith." It is also in evidence that, when faith is perfect, methods of healing are of comparatively little importance. That is to say, methods may vary within very wide limits without affecting the result, provided each patient is inspired by the requisite confidence in the particular method employed in his case. Hence the frequent successes attending each of the innumerable methods of mental healing that have prevailed in all the ages of mankind.

We have now definitely ascertained the one fundamental fact that correlates all forms, methods, and systems of mental healing. That is, we know the mental condition that must be induced in all cases, and under all systems, before mental healing becomes possible. We know that even the Master could not dispense with those conditions; for, we are told, he could not do many wonderful works among the people of his own village " because of their unbelief."

It follows that the essential thing for the healer to know is how to induce that condition in his patients. Indeed, it may be said that the whole art of mental healing consists in knowing how best to control the patient's mind in that direction. Of course there are as many ways of doing it as there are mental healers; and they are all more or less effective, as I have already stated.

This is not, however, the place to discuss the various methods in vogue. My present purpose is to point out the underlying psychological principles involved in all methods, and incidentally to show that when those principles are once comprehended, the law of mental medicine will be found to be. like all of nature's laws, simple to the last degree, and far removed from the realms of mysticism and superstition. That, for instance, which is of primary importance. namely. the induction of the essential condition of faith in the mind of the patient, .will be found to be surprisingly easy of accomplishment.

At the outset I owe an apology to many of my readers for that I shall be compelled, in this chapter, to repeat the substance of much that has been already set forth more at length in my former works.[1] This becomes necessary for the reason that the arguments in this book will be based upon the working hypothesis formulated in my first work; and although that hypothesis is now very generally accepted by scientists, it will doubtless be new to many lay readers of this treatise. In order, therefore, to make the argument comprehensible by all, its steps must be taken in orderly sequence, beginning with the fundamental psychological principles involved.

These may be stated in two propositions, namely :—

1. Man is endowed with a dual mind, or two states of consciousness. For convenience of treatment, and to make distinctions clear and readily comprehensible, I prefer to assume that man is endowed with two minds. As a working hypothesis, I am logically justified in this assumption, for the reason that everything happens just as though it were true. This fact is easily demonstrable by the processes of experimental psychology, and it is now very generally recognized by all students of psychic science.

I have chosen to designate one of the two minds as the Objective Mind and the other as the Subjective Mind, and they will be so differentiated throughout this treatise. Others have adopted other terms of differentiation, such as the " conscious " and the

---

[1] The fundamental psychological principles relating to mental healing, as well as to all other psychic phenomena, have been discussed at length in the author's work entitled " The Law of Psychic Phenomena " (A. C. McClurg & Co.).

" unconscious," the " conscious " and the " subconscious," minds, each of which is an obvious misnomer. The savants of the Society for Psychical Research generally designate the two states of consciousness as the " supraliminal " and the " subliminal," after the old psychologists. I have adopted the terms " objective " and " subjective " for the simple reason that the objective mind is the mind of ordinary waking consciousness, which takes cognizance of the objective world by means of the five objective senses; whereas the subjective mind is that intelligence which manifests itself in all subjective states and conditions, as in hypnotism, somnambulism, trance, dreams, etc., when the objective senses are asleep or are otherwise wholly or partially inhibited.

2. The second proposition is that the subjective mind is constantly amenable to control by the power of suggestion. The term "suggestion," as defined by hypnotists, signifies " the insinuation of a belief or impulse into the mind of a subject by any means, as by words or gestures, usually by emphatic declaration " (Century Dictionary). This definition is correct as far as it goes, but it is far from indicating the full scope and significance of the law of suggestion. It is not, as is indicated by the above definition, restricted to hypnotized subjects, nor to any other mental state or condition, normal or abnormal. It is a universal law of the subjective mind. The supposition that it is restricted to hypnotized subjects arose from the fact that its discoverers were studying the phenomena of hypnotism exclusively, and hence had no data for a broader generalization. It was, nevertheless, an immense stride in advance,

for it threw a flood of light upon much that was mysterious in the phenomena of hypnotism. Its chief value, however, consisted in that it paved the way for the broader discovery that it is a universal law of the subjective mind. The latter discovery was the inevitable consequence of the formulation of the doctrine of mental duality; for, it was reasoned, if man is endowed with two minds, there must necessarily be some clear line of differentiation between them, both as to their powers and their limitations. It was at length seen that suggestion and its corollaries furnished the clue to the situation. Thus, one of the corollaries of the law of suggestion is that the subjective mind is incapable of inductive reasoning; that is to say, it is incapable of instituting and conducting independently a line of research, by collecting facts, classifying them, and estimating their relative evidential values. On the contrary, it is compelled, by the primary law of its being, to accept its premises from extraneous sources; that is to say, whatever suggestions are imparted to it constitute the premises from which it reasons. It follows that its method of reasoning is purely deductive: and it is here that one of its marvellous powers is made manifest, for its power of correct deduction is well-nigh perfect. And this is true whether the premise is true or false. That is to say, its deductions from a false premise are as logically correct as from a true one; and, moreover, false and true suggestions are alike carried into active effect wherever it is possible. Thus, if it is suggested to a hypnotized subject that he is a dog, he will instantaneously assume the attitude and perform the acts of a dog, so far as it is physically possible to do so, firmly believing himself to be a dog. In a word, any character suggested, be it a fool or a philosopher, an angel or a devil, an orator or an auctioneer, will be personated with marvellous fidelity to the original, just so far as the subject's knowledge of the original extends. The wonderful histrionic ability displayed by hypnotized subjects in personating suggested characters has often been remarked. But it is not "acting a part" in the ordinary sense of the word. It is much more than acting, for the subject believes himself to be the actual personality suggested. It is not, therefore, a question of histrionic talent, in the ordinary sense; for subjects who are entirely destitute of that ability will personate to perfection any suggested character with which they are familiar. It is a common observation that excellence in the histrionic art is proportioned in each case to the actor's ability to forget his own personality and to identify himself with that of the character which he seeks to portray. It is, therefore, obvious that the whole secret of the so-called histrionic ability of the hypnotic subject is accounted for by the fact that his own personality is completely submerged under the influence of suggestion. His identification with the suggested personality is also complete, for he believes himself to be the actual person suggested. The essential prerequisite mental conditions of good acting are, therefore, present in perfection. It follows that in proportion to the subject's knowledge and intelligent appreciation of the salient characteristics of the suggested personality, will the rendition approach perfection.

It is scarcely necessary to remark that a stevedore cannot be suddenly transformed into a good actor, in the theatrical sense, by means of hypnotism. Knowledge of the salient characteristics of an individual is one thing, and knowledge of the requirements of the stage is quite another. The principle, however, is the same. It follows that an actor who has intelligently studied his part and knows its requirements, but is deficient in the power of rendition, could be trained to a high state of efficiency in the histrionic art by means of hypnotic suggestion. It would, of course, require a trainer of high character and exceptional intelligence to achieve the best results.[1]

I mention these hypnotic experiments for the purpose of showing how perfectly the subjective mind is dominated by the power of suggestion. Whether true or false, a suggestion wields a potent influence, although there are necessarily degrees of potency depending upon conditions, just as there are degrees of potency under varying conditions in every force in nature. And, like every other force in nature, suggestion acts most effectively on lines of least resistance. Thus, a suggestion that is contrary to the moral principles of the subject will be resisted with a strength and persistence proportioned to its moral obliquity. A suggestion the performance of which

[1] Since the above was written, Dr. John Duncan Quackenbos, emeritus professor of Psychology in Columbia University, read a paper before the Medico-Legal Society of New York on this subject, which has since been published in the "Medico-Legal Journal." The doctor is one of the leading hypnotists in this country; and he reports some marvellous successes in training actors for the stage. Prof A. E. Carpenter, of Boston, has also been highly successful in training subjects for the lecture platform.

would render the subject an object of ridicule will be resisted by him with an emphasis proportioned to his pride and dignity. A suggestion that would imperil the life of the subject if carried into execution will be resisted with an energy proportioned to the degree and imminence of the peril involved.

These do not constitute exceptions to the law of suggestion. On the contrary, they serve to illustrate its universality. For, be it remembered, an auto-suggestion is just as potent, other things being equal, as a suggestion from another person; and when the subjective mind is confronted by two opposing suggestions, the stronger one necessarily prevails. Thus, the settled moral principles of the subject's life will successfully resist the suggestions of crime or immorality; for moral principles constitute auto-suggestions, the strength of which is proportioned to that of his moral character. The subject's dignity of character, in like manner, constitutes an auto-suggestion that may successfully resist a suggestion the active acceptance of which would place him in a ridiculous attitude; and the instinct of self-preservation will, on the same principle, cause him to refuse to imperil his life.

There are, in fact, an infinite number of conditions which tend more or less strongly to modify or divert the force of the suggestions which find lodgment in the subjective mind of man. Thus, a suggestion that is known by the subject in his normal condition to be absolutely false will always excite at least a momentary opposition, and that, too, will be duly proportioned to the enormity of the falsehood.

In matters of indifference to him he may be induced, by persistence and iteration, to accept and act upon it; or where the performance of the act suggested promises to result in a decided advantage to himself, he may accept it with alacrity. In any event, when a suggestion is once accepted and followed by corresponding action, its falsity and its incongruities are soon lost sight of by the subject, and, to all its possible intents and purposes, it becomes a reality to his subjective mind; and it is followed by all its consequences, within the limits of physical possibility. Practical illustrations of this are often seen in certain systems of mental therapeutics, where the patient is told that if he will consent to believe certain things that he knows to be untrue and to the last degree absurd and impossible, his faith will be speedily followed by restored health. Resistance to such a suggestion is, of course, instantaneous; and it is prolonged in proportion to the patient's intelligence. Nevertheless, many marvellous cures have resulted under suggestions that to the alienist clearly reveal their origin in a pathological condition of the mind of their inventor.

It will now be seen that the effectiveness of suggestions is not dependent upon the induction of the hypnotic condition; for under the system to which allusion has been made that condition is never induced, that is, in the sense in which hypnosis is commonly understood. That is to say, the condition of hypnotic sleep is never induced. Passivity of mind and body is all that is required of the patients, which, as we shall see later on, is the equivalent of hypnosis for therapeutic purposes.

The points to be observed and remembered in connection with the foregoing are the following: —

1. The subjective mind is constantly amenable to control by suggestion without reference to the state or condition of the objective mind.

2. Suggestions operate most effectively on lines of least resistance.

3. Resistance to suggestions from extraneous sources arises from auto-suggestions having their origin in various emotions, such as the primordial instincts (as of self-preservation, love of offspring, etc.), settled moral principles, sensitiveness to ridicule, fixed habits of thought, or love of scientific truth. This includes resistance to suggestions which are in obvious contravention of reason, experience, or the evidence of the senses.

4. Resistance to the last-named suggestions is proportioned to the intelligence of the subject, and hence it is often overcome by persistence, especially when accompanied by promises of resultant benefits, as in certain methods of mental healing.

It follows that while the faith that is required to make therapeutic suggestions effective is primarily the faith of the subjective mind, nevertheless suggestions are most potent when they are not antagonized by any resistance whatever, either intellectual or emotional. Hence it is that suggestions which are based upon scientific truth, other things being equal, are necessarily the most potent in their influence and permanent in their effects. As in all the other relations of human life, truth is mightier than error or falsehood, and it is the condition precedent to all permanent good.

Having now briefly outlined the salient points pertaining to the first two fundamental psychological propositions, it remains to add a third term to complete a working hypothesis for the systematic study of mental medicine. The third term, or proposition, therefore, is that *The subjective mind is the power that controls the functions, sensations, and conditions of the body.*

I need not dwell at length upon this proposition here, as its truth will more fully appear as we proceed in subsequent chapters. No scientist will deny the existence within us of a central intelligence which controls the bodily functions, and, through the sympathetic nervous system, actuates the involuntary muscles, and keeps the bodily machinery in motion. Nor will the most pronounced materialist deny that this central intelligence is the controlling energy which regulates the action of each of the myriad cellular entities of which the whole body is composed. It matters not how we may designate it, or what our theories may be as to its origin and destiny; it exists. Whether we call it the " principle of life," the " abdominal brain," the " communal soul," the " subliminal consciousness," or the " subjective mind," it exists; and it controls the bodily functions in health and disease, and, in turn, is controllable by the subtle power of suggestion.

We have, then, in three propositions, each of which is demonstrable by experimentation, a complete working hypothesis for the systematic study and practice of mental therapeutics. They may be restated and grouped in systematic order as follows: —

1. Man is endowed with a dual mind, — objective and subjective.

2. The subjective mind controls the functions, sensations, and conditions of the body.

3. The subjective mind is amenable to control by suggestion.

CHAPTER III

THE VARIOUS SYSTEMS OF MENTAL HEALING

The Intelligence that controls the Functions of the Body in Health the
Power or Energy that requires Assistance in Case of Disease. —
The Body a Confederation of Micro-organisms controlled by this
Central Intelligence. — It is a Mental Organism that all Therapeutic Agencies are designed to energize — Mental Therapeutic Agencies the Primary and Normal Means for this End. — Physical
Agencies not excluded — A Mental Stimulus more direct and
positive than a Physical One. — Material Remedies Good and
Legitimate Forms of Suggestion. — Whether Remedies are Material or Mental, they must energize the Central Controlling Intelligence. — The Therapeutic Value of all Agencies proportioned to
their Power to stimulate the Subjective Mind. — Suggestion the
Prepotent Therapeutic Energy. — This is the Law of Mental Healing. — The Teleological Argument to be drawn from the Law of
Mental Medicine. — None other so demonstrative of Divine Benevolence. — Absence of Fear and Pain at the Moment of Dissolution. — This Phenomena, considered together with the Law of
Mental Healing, possesses a Teleological Significance. — The Law
of Mental Healing is universal and adapted to every Grade of
Human Intelligence. — Antiquity of Suggestion as a Therapeutic
Agent. — Its Myriad Forms. — All effective in proportion to their
Faith-Inspiring Potency — Scientific Significance of the Beliefs
and Practices of Primitive Humanity. — All were useful, and
each was adapted to some Special Grade of Intelligence. — Primitive Minds still exist in the Highest Modern Civilization with
Corresponding Powers of Reasoning. — Current Beliefs adapted
to Varying Grades of Intelligence. — Their Religious Features
Potent Factors in their Success. — Systems based upon Error less
efficacious than one founded upon Truth. — Nearly all refer the
Healing Power to Extraneous Sources, an Error which Jesus insistently controverted.

IT must now be evident to the scientific student
that the three propositions stated at the close of
the preceding chapter apply with equal force to every
system of mental medicine, from fetichism to the
most exact and scientific system of suggestive therapeutics. Like all the laws of nature, the law of
mental medicine is universal in its application; and,
like all the others, it is simple and easily comprehended. Granted that there is an intelligence that
controls the functions of the body in health, it follows that it is the same power or energy that fails
in case of disease. Failing, it requires assistance;
and that is what all therapeutic agencies aim to accomplish. No intelligent physician of any school
claims to be able to do more than to "assist nature"
to restore normal conditions of the body. That it is
a mental energy that thus requires assistance, no one
denies: for science teaches us that the whole body
is made up of a confederation of intelligent entities,
each of which performs its functions with an intelligence exactly adapted to the performance of its
special duties as a member of the confederacy. There
is, indeed, no life without mind, from the lowest unicellular organism up to man. It is, therefore, a mental energy that actuates every fibre of the body under
all its conditions. That there is a central intelligence
that controls each of those mind organisms, is self-
evident. Whether, as the materialistic scientists insist, this central intelligence is merely the sum of all
the cellular intelligences of the bodily organism, or
is an independent entity, capable of sustaining a separate existence after the body perishes, is a question
that does not concern us in the pursuance of the pres-

ent inquiry. It is sufficient for us to know that such an intelligence exists, and that, for the time being, it is the controlling energy that normally regulates the action of the myriad cells of which the body is composed.

It is, then, a mental organism that all therapeutic agencies are designed to energize, when, for any cause, it fails to perform its functions with reference to any part of the physical structure. It follows that mental therapeutic agencies are the primary and normal means of energizing that mental organism. That is to say, mental agencies operate more directly than any other, because more intelligibly, upon a mental organism; although physical agencies are by no means excluded, for all experience shows that a mental organism responds to physical as well as to mental stimuli. All that can be reasonably claimed is that, in therapeutics, a mental stimulus is necessarily more direct and more positive in its effects, other things being equal, than a physical stimulus can be, for the simple reason that it is intelligent on the one hand and intelligible on the other. It must be remarked, however, that it is obviously impossible wholly to eliminate mental suggestion even in the administration of material remedies. Extremists claim that the whole effect of material remedies is due to the factor of mental suggestion; but this seems to be untenable, for reasons stated in another chapter. The most that can be claimed with any degree of certainty is that material remedies, when they are not in themselves positively injurious, are good and legitimate forms of suggestion, and, as such, are invested with a certain therapeutic potency, as in the administration of the placebo. It is also certain that, whether the remedies are material or mental, they must, directly or indirectly, energize the mental organism in control of the bodily functions. Otherwise the therapeutic effects produced cannot be permanent. It follows that the therapeutic value of all remedial agencies, material or mental, is proportioned to their respective powers to produce the effect of stimulating the subjective mind to a state of normal activity, and directing its energies into appropriate channels. We know that suggestion fills this requirement more directly and positively than any other known therapeutic agent; and this is all that needs to be done for the restoration of health in any case outside the domain of surgery. It is all that can be done. No power in the universe can do more than energize the mental organism that is the seat and source of health within the body. A miracle could do no more.

This, then, is a law of mental healing. Is there any other? Each of the indefinite number of sects of mental healers now in evidence in this country tells us that it has a law of its own, — which is the only genuine article, all the others being either feeble imitations or wholly fraudulent, wicked, and diabolical. They agree in but one thing, and that is in hating the medical profession; and they hate but one thing more than they do that profession, and that is each other. They have, however, a common logic, by means of which each one proves that his is the only scientific system of mental therapeutics. Each holds that the fact that he heals the sick by his method is demonstrative that his theory is the criterion of scientific truth. I have before remarked that the one thing that correlates all methods of mental healing is the fact that they all succeed in healing disease. If, therefore, their logic is sound, there are as many laws of mental medicine as there are mental healers; and the " systems " of the Black-foot Indian and the fetich worshipper stand on as firm a scientific basis as the most enlightened mental therapeutist of the twentieth century.

It requires but the most elementary scientific education to teach one to know that God is not thus prodigal of special laws. The first lesson that the merest tyro in science learns is that all of nature's laws are general, that each one covers a vast domain, and that allied or cognate phenomena are governed by some one universal law which tolerates no exceptions. In nothing is the wisdom of the Creator so conspicuously manifested as in the universality of his laws; and theology has never formulated a teleological argument so strong and convincing and unanswerable as that to be drawn from the law of mental medicine. For it not only shows the infinite wisdom of God, but it is demonstrative of his infinite love for all mankind, his infinite mercy, his infinite benevolence toward all sentient creatures. All the laws of nature may be said to exhibit infinite intelligence and wisdom: but they do not all demonstrate, to the finite understanding, the existence of the attributes of love, mercy, and benevolence in the character of the Lawgiver. The law of organic evolution. for instance, involves an infinite prodigality of life, and the necessity for universal death, to say nothing of the apparently total disregard of the lives and the comfort of all sentient creatures involved in the normal operation of the physical forces of nature. It requires the postulation of a design, a commensurate end in view, — namely, the development of man, the evolution of an immortal soul, — to make the wisdom of the law of organic evolution manifest to the common understanding. To those, however, who choose to deny the existence of any such evidences of design, the structure of the physical universe and the display of its physical forces prove nothing but the existence of a blind, unintelligent energy, actuated by an iron necessity, in which man figures as an accidental and altogether insignificant product. To be entirely candid, it must be admitted that when the physical forces of nature are alone considered, the atheistic view is not without a basis of reason. But when we consider in this connection the phenomena of mind, as exhibited in all sentient creatures, from the lowest unicellular organism up to man, the argument falls of its own weight. It is true that much in the phenomena of mind may be accounted for by reference to the law of heredity and the accidents of environment, but not all. Heredity may be invoked to account for all that is thus transmissible, and environment may account for modifications; but there are attributes of all sentient life which heredity cannot explain and which environment cannot modify. For instance, the immunity from fear of death on its near approach, or when it becomes inevitable, is a blessing that is enjoyed by all sentient creatures. And those physicians who are most familiar with death in all its forms assure us that in the process of dissolution no pain whatever is experienced. On the contrary, the sensations are evidently pleasurable rather than painful. At least, no matter what form death may assume, all fear of it vanishes upon its near approach, and the victim dies " without pain and without regret " (Hammond).

Now, no one has ever been able to assign a biological reason for this immunity. It stands apart from all other biological facts in that it appears to be valueless as a factor in the scheme of organic evolution, and yet it is as universal as sentient life itself. The fear of death is also universal; but it has its uses, which are obvious, as is the universal instinct of reproduction. Pain is also useful as a preservative of life, in that it stands as a sentinel to warn sentient creatures of imminent peril. But of what practical utility, from a biological point of view, is immunity from physical pain and mental agony, when the supreme moment arrives? It neither prolongs life nor shortens it for an instant, nor does it affect in the remotest degree the welfare of those that are left behind. Its only importance, therefore, pertains to the individual who experiences the sensation. Brief as it is, it is of supreme importance to him.

It is idle to say that a fact in nature so universal as this, is without commensurate significance: and since biological explanations fail we are driven to seek for ethical reasons. Nor are they hard to find if we postulate a God of infinite love, mercy, and benevolence toward his creatures, and yet a God whose reign is of law. The law of evolution necessitates a struggle for life, ending in inevitable death. Without the struggle there could be no improvement, no progressive development. Without universal death evolution would cease in a generation. Since, therefore, all must die, is it not an appropriate measure of compensation or mitigation, to rob death of its terrors and its agony? It is, indeed, the only conceivable mitigation of the death penalty; and human lawgivers in civilized countries exhaust the resources of science in an effort to devise means to insure a painless death for those whom the law has condemned to die. The quality of mercy thus evinced in human enactments is obviously identical in kind and purpose with the divine. It follows that the same logical conclusions are derivable from both, namely: *A law that produces exclusively the results of mercy and benevolence, presupposes a lawgiver who is endowed with intelligence and actuated by corresponding emotions.*

The pious Jacobi[1] once said in effect, " Nature conceals God; man reveals God." This is eminently true as far as it goes, but it does not go far enough. If he had said that *mind* alone reveals God, he would have included all the indubitable revelations of the existence of an intelligent Deity that the universe affords: for the mind of the lowest unicellular organism presents evidence as conclusive of its divine origin as is found in the mind of man.[2] If he had said that God reveals himself unmistakably to man only in the sign-language of love, mercy, and benevolence, he would have expressed a great scientific truth.

---

[1] Quoted by Sir William Hamilton, Metaphysics, p. 29.
[2] See " The Divine Pedigree of Man."

Cognate to these phenomena, in their beneficent characteristics, are those of mental healing. One is for the benefit of the dying, and the other of the living. Considered separately, the phenomena of mental healing do not possess equal teleological significance with the phenomena immediately accompanying dissolution, because the former may be considered merely as a part of the grand scheme by which life is conserved and evolution is made possible. Considered together, however, as all cognate phenomena must be considered, the evidential value of one series is carried over into the other. Hence we have a logical right to regard the qualities of mercy and benevolence, which are inseparable from the law of mental healing, as possessing equal teleological significance with the same qualities in the other class of phenomena.

It is, however, no part of my purpose to formulate a teleological argument, *per se,* in this connection. I merely wish to draw attention to the grand scheme of benevolence to mankind involved in the law of mental healing. Whether we consider it a purposive scheme of benevolence on the part of an intelligent Deity, or as the accidental outcome of the operation of blind and unintelligent forces reacting upon each other, — that is to say, whether we consider it as a law of God or a law of nature, — the law exists; and its effects are those of infinite mercy and benevolence toward all mankind. The laws of physical nature excite emotions of admiration and awe, and even reverence; but they are tempered by the reflection that in their phenomenal manifestations they regard not the well-being or the life of man, and that the most sublime manifestation of nature's forces may be surcharged with irresistible ruin and death to thousands of human beings. On the other hand, the law of mental healing stimulates equally the emotions of admiration, reverence. love. and gratitude, — admiration and reverence for its universality and its wisdom; love, for that behind it the Divine Father stands revealed; and gratitude, for that, in all its effects, his infinite love, mercy, and benevolence are made manifest.

From a scientific point of view there is nothing in the broad realm of natural law that is more truly wonderful than the law of mental healing. Its simplicity has already been shown: and this alone is *prima facie* evidence of the validity of the three psychological propositions which constitute its formula. And, as in every other law of nature, this *prima facie* evidence becomes conclusive proof when the fact of universality is established. It is the fact of the universality of this law that excites the wonder and extorts the admiration of the scientist, for the reason that it is adapted to every conceivable grade of human intelligence, from that of primitive savagery to that of the highest conceivable civilization. It is impossible to find words in which to express adequately the value to mankind of this stupendous fact. We may faintly realize it, however, when we reflect that for untold ages suggestion was the only therapeutic agency available to man. Medicine, if we date its advent from Hippocrates, "the father of medicine," who flourished about 400 B. C., is a modern institution when compared with that long line of healers who wrought their therapeutic wonders by the aid of suggestion in its myriad forms.

It would require many volumes of the size of this to catalogue the different methods of mental healing, ancient and modern, and point out how suggestion operates to effect a cure in each particular case. Nor is it necessary to do so; for the intelligent reader has already grasped the central idea that any form of belief which inspires the faith of the patient, when supplemented by a corresponding therapeutic suggestion, is efficacious as a therapeutic agency. In other words, conditions being favorable, anything that the patient has faith in is efficacious as a therapeutic agent. Thus, the fetich worshipper, who believes that a stick or a stone is inhabited by a powerful and beneficent spirit whose aid can be invoked by certain ceremonies, may, by the performance of the prescribed rites, be restored to health. Why? Simply because the ceremony constitutes a suggestion which inspires the faith and stimulates into normal activity and energy that central intelligence which controls the bodily functions. The North American Indian believes that evil spirits are responsible for all his diseases; and his medicine man tells him that he can frighten away said evil spirits by making hideous noises, supplemented by a diabolical make-up. He prepares himself accordingly, and seating himself before the wigwam door, in full view of the patient, proceeds to make things unpleasant for all concerned, and positively unendurable for the evil spirit. The latter generally flees in the course of a day or two, leaving the patient to recover. I have authentic information from educated Indians, who assure me that, for " the poor Indian, whose untutored mind sees God in clouds or hears him in the wind," this method of healing is generally more effective than are the material remedies of the educated physician. It is scarcely necessary to remark that the suggestion embraced in his belief as to the cause of disease, together with the performance of the ceremony which he believed to be an effective way of removing the cause, was the all-sufficient therapeutic agency in the case of the North American Indian.

It is obvious that the same remarks apply to all conceivable theories of causation and all forms of suggestion corresponding to the theories. They are all effective in exact proportion to their faith-inspiring potency. It is not surprising, therefore, that in the days of primitive humanity, when superstition was universal, there prevailed an indefinite number of effective methods of mental healing.

Nor does it become the scientists of this enlightened age to scoff at the primitive beliefs and practices of humanity in its infancy. It was the only therapeutic agency that was available to them; and if they builded better than they knew, it was because God, in his infinite mercy, had instituted a law adapted to the therapeutic uses of every grade of human intelligence. It is equally reprehensible for us to inveigh against any of the innumerable systems of mental healing that prevail amidst the highest civilization of the twentieth century. They are all useful, and they are useful simply because each one is adapted to some special grade of intelligence. Besides, it must not be forgotten that primitive minds. with corresponding methods of thought and powers of reasoning, still exist in vast numbers in this as in all previous ages of mankind. It is, indeed, doubtful if primitive man ever entertained a superstitious belief that was more gross and grotesque than some that prevail at the present day and form the basis of popular and successful systems of mental therapeutics. Between the grossest superstition and scientific truth there necessarily exist many gradations of human intelligence; and the fact that all grades exist together in the most civilized nations is due to the fact that civilization itself is still in the formative stage. As the phylogenetic history of the primordial germ is repeated, step by step, in the ontogenetic history of the germinal cell of man. so is every grade of the progressive development of civilization to be found existing together in the most enlightened nations. It follows that variant theories and systems of mental healing are as likely to prevail now as they were in the days of primitive man. Accordingly we find a great and constantly increasing number of systems, each with an enthusiastic following. This could not be true were it not for the fact that they are all more or less successful mental healers. They could not be successful mental healers were they not able to induce the necessary mental conditions in their patients; and they could not induce the necessary conditions with any certainty of uniform results, were their systems, respectively, not adapted to the mental capacity of their followers. That is to say, the theory of causation and the form of suggestion in each case must, in order to produce the best results, appeal to the beliefs, the habits of thought, or the prejudices of the patient; which is but another way of saying, what has already been dwelt upon, that suggestions are most effective when acting upon lines of least resistance.

It is true that the faith required for therapeutic purposes is the faith of the subjective mind; and, as that mind is controllable by the power of suggestion, it may be thus controlled even when the basic theory of causation is contrary to reason, experience, and the evidence of the senses. But in such cases some emotion that is stronger in the mind of the patient than the mere love of scientific truth must be appealed to in order to make a therapeutic suggestion effective. Thus, a strong desire or hope of renewed health will cause many to ignore all theories which may be entertained by the healer, however imbecile they may be; and by dissociating the therapeutic suggestion from the theory of causation, they will be able to experience the benefits of the suggestion. This is comparatively easy for one who has had no scientific training, or in whom the love of scientific truth is subordinate to the egoistic emotions. The religious emotions are also potent factors in causing many to ignore an impossible theory, or even to believe it with hysterical fervency, when they are told that the theory is inseparable from successful practice.

Besides, there is a large class of people in every community the fervency of whose belief in theories that minister to their emotions is always in inverse proportion to the amount of evidence that can be adduced to sustain them. Hence it happens that those theories which command their most fervent belief, and are advocated with hysterical aggressiveness, are invariably those which everybody knows to be untrue.

Nevertheless, their system is exactly adapted to their mental capacity; and, speaking from a purely therapeutical standpoint, they are entitled to the undisturbed enjoyment of their beliefs and the benefits derivable therefrom. The law of mental healing is as clearly for their benefit as it is for all other classes of people and grades of human intelligence. There is, indeed, a therapeutic value to them in being undisturbed in their beliefs; for experience shows that the efficacy of a therapeutic suggestion is weakened, and often destroyed, by disturbing the prejudices of the patient. Thus, it often happens that after a cure has been effected, the patient will totally relapse upon learning that the healer believes something against which the patient entertains a prejudice, or disbelieves in something which the patient believes, although the belief or the disbelief may not have the remotest connection with mental healing. This is especially true of religious beliefs and prejudices. Hence it was that the Master always carefully avoided disturbing the religious prejudices or beliefs of his patients.

It is, therefore, worse than useless, from a therapeutic point of view, to attempt to educate one of the classes referred to in the true science of mental therapeutics. As a rule, they have never been trained in scientific methods of investigation or in habits of clear thinking; and a palpable fact is considered by them as utterly valueless when it conflicts with some fantastical theory that ministers to their emotions. Besides, those who have sought to make a religion of mental healing are doing a good work; for, besides healing the sick, they have poured the balm of religious consolation into many a stricken heart, and made better men and women of many who were unable to assimilate any other form of religion. This is but another way of saying that their religion is adapted to the needs and capacity of those who can assimilate it. I have said that mental healing is not a religion, and for that statement I have the authority of the Master; but that is not saying that true religion is not a powerful auxiliary to mental healing. All experience shows that it is; for it is not only a wonderfully efficacious form of suggestion, but it promotes that calm serenity of mind which is of the first importance in all systems of mental medicine. Prayer is also wonderfully effective, for more reasons than one; but this subject cannot be discussed here.

But, while mental healing is in no sense a religion, it is impossible for any right-minded person to reflect upon the law of mental healing, its universality, its adaptability to all grades of human intelligence, together with its implications of divine love, mercy, and benevolence, without a feeling of the profoundest reverence for the Being whose wisdom and fatherhood is thus unmistakably manifested. It teaches humility, promotes religion, inspires gratitude, and disarms prejudice against any form or process by which the law is made available for the alleviation of human suffering.

It must not be inferred from the foregoing that

all systems of mental healing are of equal value to mankind, for that would be equivalent to alleging that error and superstition are as potent for good as scientific truth. God has not thus equalized the value of truth and falsehood, or good and evil, for any purpose whatever. In primitive times, when all systems were based upon error, they may have been equally valuable as instruments of God's mercy to his children during the infancy of the human race, when truth was not available to any. But in an enlightened age, when many are seeking for truth with strenuous effort, and some are even finding it, the whole aspect is changed; for when once a fundamental truth is discovered, in any science, or in any field of human thought, all systems based upon error must eventually yield, however useful they may have been in their day and generation. Nothing is permanent but truth. Error loses its vitality in the sunlight of truth; and hence no human institution that is based upon a fundamental error can permanently endure in the presence of a fundamental truth. Wrong systems may endure for ages when sustained by interest or prejudice; but their incidental good effects become less and less in evidence, and finally vanish. This is especially true in the domain of mind, where everything depends upon mental attitudes and conditions.

I have already shown how the effects of a valid therapeutic suggestion may be vitiated by the emotional prejudices of the patient. It is obvious that the same effect is likely to happen when a patient has been healed by a false system and afterwards learns that the system is based upon a fundamental

error. Action and reaction are always equal. Hence.
when a lover of truth reacts against a false system,
the violence of the reaction is proportioned to the
grotesque imbecility of the system. He simply loses
faith in the false system when he learns the truth;
and the effects are retroactive. It is obvious that
there can be no such reaction against a system
founded upon scientific truth. Reaction against an
inductive science is impossible, for truth is eternal.
Every step, therefore, is in advance; for every fresh
discovery of fundamental truth forms the basis of
a new departure into still higher realms of the same
truth and its cognates. The reaction is. therefore,
always against error when truth is once discovered
and made manifest to the human understanding.

There is, however, another reason for the want of
permanency in the cures effected under false theories
of causation. All, or nearly all, of them refer the
power that effects the healing to some agency extraneous to the patient himself. This, as I have already
pointed out. is a fundamental error which Jesus com-
bated with insistent iteration. It is not only false
as a matter of demonstrable fact, but it is the pro-
genitor of a whole train of false theories and conclusions, some of which contain the germs of a
destructive energy that is often fatal to the permanency of the cures effected under the hypothesis.
The reason is that when a patient is once convinced
that an extraneous power has interposed to effect
his cure, he feels that he is in some way dependent
upon that power for the future preservation of his
health. He feels himself to be a helpless dependent
upon the favor of some extraneous intelligence of

which he knows nothing, except that its aid was once invoked in his behalf by some third person, namely, the healer. The result is that when the personality of the healer is removed, the patient begins to entertain doubts as to whether he may expect a continuance of the favor. Soon his doubts deepen into convictions, and when the expected unfavorable symptoms are felt, his convictions become certainties, and he feels that for some inscrutable reason he has forfeited the good-will of the healing agency. The result is a relapse. In one form or another this adverse factor is ever present with him who heeds not the words of the Master, but pins his faith upon some hypothetical healing power extraneous to himself, and whose favor he cannot command.

All this is, of course, in violent contrast to the true science of mental healing as it has been deduced from the immutable laws of nature recently discovered by modern scientists. Of the existence of those laws there can be no room for rational doubt. They have been demonstrated by thousands of the most careful scientific experiments by the ablest living psychologists. Their universal applicability to the phenomena of mental healing has also been demonstrated by careful observation and experimentation. That is to say, the existence of those psychological laws affords a scientific explanation of all the phenomena of mental healing. It shows why each and all methods are successful in the production of therapeutic results.

The fact remains that there can be but one correct method — or, to say the least, but one best method — of applying the law to the uses of mental medicine. That method must necessarily be the one which is based upon demonstrable scientific truth: the method which eliminates all taint of fraud, falsehood, and superstition; the method which appeals to the reason of both healer and patient. The faith of the patient being the primary mental condition sought, it is obviously more easily attained by an appeal to reason than to blind credulity. The effects are more permanent because there can never be a reaction against it caused by a discovery of fraud, deception, or a false suggestion. It is also more permanent because the science teaches man what he is. It reveals his inherent powers and points out his limitations. Most important of all in this connection is the fact that, in revealing man to himself, it teaches him that he can control the energy within himself which, in turn, controls his vital functions.

These remarks apply, of course, only to those who love truth better than falsehood or error, and who are mentally capable of exercising the discriminative power of induction; and they are not addressed to any other class of minds.

CHAPTER IV

THE DUPLEX MENTAL ORGANISM

Faith can be acquired by Study and Reasoning. — Thus acquired, it is perfect and permanent. — It is essential that the Healer be grounded in the Fundamental Principles of his Science. — The Phenomena of Dreams point to the Theory of the Dual Mind. — The Operations of the Dream Intelligence essentially different from those of Waking Consciousness. — The Subjective, or Dream Intelligence incapable of Inductive Reasoning, and controlled by Suggestion. — Rapidity of Subjective Mentation. — Hypnotism a Means by which Dreams can be induced, controlled, and experimented with. — It is the Instrument for the Investigation of the Problems of Psychology. — It has found in Man a Soul, and revealed the Evidence of its Divine Origin. — It has segregated the Phenomena of the Objective and Subjective Minds, and shown the Distinctive Powers and Limitations of Each.

HAVING now stated in general outline the fundamental principles of mental medicine, and shown the universality of the law of nature under which is made possible the healing of the nations, it remains to deal more in detail with the fundamental propositions which constitute the basis of scientific mental healing. This becomes necessary for the reason that success in mental healing by scientific methods is best promoted by first acquiring a clear understanding of the law under which the healing is effected. In other words, scientific methods require scientific knowledge for their successful application. It is scarcely necessary to observe that this is in violent contrast to the conditions required for success in mental healing by the unscientific methods to which we have alluded in the preceding chapter. Obviously a knowledge of science, or a capacity to reason, would handicap a healer who practises by methods involving an unscientific theory of causation, especially one that involves the insensate denial of every fact of human experience.

Nevertheless, faith is as essential to success in healing by scientific methods as by any other. But there are three advantages in this regard which are incident to scientific methods. The first is that the requisite faith can be acquired by study and reasoning; the second is that the faith is perfect, for the reason that it is acquired through knowledge and confirmed by reason; and the third is that the faith thus acquired and sanctioned becomes at once a permanent possession, because there can arise no adverse auto-suggestions from the objective mind to weaken its potency.

It becomes, therefore, a matter of the first importance for the healer to be well grounded in the fundamental principles underlying the science which he proposes to utilize; for he should be able to instruct his patients in its fundamentals, to the end that he may be filled with the same kind and quality of faith that the healer possesses. — the faith born of knowledge of the law, and not of blind credulity. Otherwise he would enjoy no advantage not possessed by the fetich worshipper.

I shall, therefore, dwell at some length upon the evidence demonstrative of the truth of each of the terms of our hypothesis, and incidentally upon some of the practical uses of the law in affairs of every-day life.

First, then, of the duplex mental organism.

Every one who has had a dream has in some measure realized the duplex character of his own mind. He knows that the brain is the organ of the mind of ordinary waking consciousness; but he knows that in sleep the brain is quiescent, — that, in fact, sleep is the condition in which that organ rests and recuperates. Yet he realizes that during that period of brain rest there is a mental energy in evidence that seems to act independently of the mind with whose normal operations he is acquainted. He can sometimes trace a connection between his waking thoughts and his dreams; but he frequently realizes that the latter correspond to no possible human experience. At other times he becomes conscious of the presence of a mental energy which far transcends that of his normal experience or capacity,—a mind which can solve mathematical problems that are beyond the compass of his normal powers. Again he becomes conscious that his dream intelligence is filled with the most sublime thoughts and is capable of clothing them in the most beautiful and appropriate language, — language that is far beyond his normal linguistic powers, — thoughts which were strangers to his normal consciousness. Sometimes the key to the most profound secrets of nature are thus revealed to him, and are thus made available for normal uses and practical exploitation. Again, dreams often reveal an apparent independence, on the part of the dream intelligence, of the space and time limitations with which one is normally acquainted. Thus, it is not uncommon for one to become aware, by means of dreams, of what is happening to his near relatives and friends who are thousands of miles distant, with no possible means of communication between them through sensory channels. He thus becomes aware that his dream intelligence possesses powers and facilities for receiving and cognizing intelligence from others not possessed by his normal intelligence.

These facts alone seem to point to the theory of duality as a rational solution of the phenomena. But when we consider the limitations of the dream intelligence, we find still stronger evidence to the same effect. Thus, we find that it is constantly amenable to control by suggestion. This, too, is within the range of every one's experience. Everybody is aware that the dream intelligence never realizes the incongruity of the most ridiculously impossible dream situations. No fact of human experience weighs one hair against the suggestions arising from the sensations caused by an overloaded stomach. Reason abdicates her throne in the presence of the vision of one's grandmother sporting seven heads and ten horns, and mounted upon a fiery and untamed saw-horse. The dreamer is neither surprised at the conduct of his grandmother nor at the character of her mount, and he never suspects that she is possessed of more than a normal number of heads and horns.

It is obvious, therefore, that the dream intelligence is devoid of the power of inductive reasoning, — which is but another way of saying that it is controlled by suggestion. And this we find it to be to a very remarkable degree. Thus, in a case cited by Abercrombie,[1] a bottle of hot water at the feet of the dreamer caused him to dream of walking on the warm ground near the crater of Mount Ætna. Another, whose bed-clothes were accidentally thrown off during the night in a cold room, dreamed of spending the winter at Hudson's Bay, and of suffering much from the intense frost.[2] It is needless, however, to multiply cases, as few are exempt from such experiences.

These phenomena can be accounted for on no other rational hypothesis than that of duality of mind. Two states of consciousness are certainly in evidence; and the phenomena are radically different, each from the other. So radical, indeed, are the differences, in both powers and limitations, between the waking and the dream intelligences, that we are justified in assuming, for the purposes of a working hypothesis, that there are two separable, and therefore distinct, intelligences in man's mental organism. That there is a nexus between the two that enables them to act in perfect synchronism when occasion requires, is necessarily true. It is to this synchronism of action that we are indebted for what is designated as "genius." It is also in evidence on occasions of great importance to the individual, as when danger is imminent, or some great crisis is impending.[3]

---

[1] Intellectual Powers, p. 216.

[2] Op. cit., p. 216.

[3] For a full discussion of these subjects, see "The Law of Psychic Phenomena."

There are other phenomena of dreams of great evidential importance, though less distinctly pointing to duality. The one about to be mentioned exhibits powers of inconceivably rapid mentation possessed by the dream intelligence. Dreams that are induced by percussive sounds, more frequently than any others, display this phenomenon in perfection. Thus. Professor Carpenter, of Boston. relates the following illustrative experience: The professor was at the house of a friend, and slept in a bedroom the door of which opened outward into the hall. It stood open during the night: and in the morning some one opened a window at the end of the hall, letting in a draught of air that shut the professor's door with great violence. He instantly awoke. — so quickly. in fact. that when fully awake he realized the cause of the concussion. In the meantime, however, he dreamed a dream the events of which would have required nearly a year of time in the happening. It was during the progress of the late civil war, and at a time when conscription was the order of the day. He dreamed that the dreaded order came, and his name was on the list. He tried to get it removed. but an examination demonstrated his eligibility; and when the drawing came off, his name, like Abou Ben Adhem's, " led all the rest." He then set to work to hire a substitute. But the fates were against him. When he could get a man, he could not raise the money; and when at last he raised the money, he could not find an eligible man. Finally, he was hustled into a uniform that did not fit, and was then transported to the State rendezvous, where he spent three miserable months in drilling in the awkward squad. At the end of that time his regiment was ordered to Washington, where another three months was spent in acquiring a military education. He was then ordered to the front, where he was forced to endure the hardships of camp life for an indefinite period. In the midst of his monotonous misery he suddenly became aware that he was in the hottest part of a great battle. He was awakened to the realization of the situation by the sudden firing of a cannon, or the bursting of a shell, in his immediate vicinity. It was the slamming of the door that awoke him at once to a realization of his objective and his subjective surroundings.

Abercrombie [1] relates a similar case that happened in Edinburgh at a period when there was an alarm of French invasion, and almost every man in the city was a soldier. All things had been arranged in expectation of the landing of an enemy; the first notice of which was to be given by a gun from the castle. The gentleman to whom the dream occurred, and who had been a most zealous volunteer, was in bed between two and three o'clock in the morning, when he dreamed of hearing the signal gun. He was immediately at the castle, witnessed the proceedings for displaying the signals that had been planned for arousing the whole surrounding country, and saw and heard a great bustle over the town from troops and artillery assembling, especially in Princes Street. At this time he was roused by his wife, who awoke in a fright caused by a similar dream, connected with much noise and the

[1] Op. cit., p. 217.

landing of an enemy. The origin of this remarkable concurrence was ascertained, in the morning, to be the noise produced by the fall of a pair of tongs upon the floor above.[1]

Many similar cases are related by the old psychologists, some of the dreams involving years of dream-time. The salient features of this class of dreams, to which attention is invited. are, first. that the sound that awakens the sleeper is identical with the sound that forms the culminating feature of the dream. This, of course, involves the apparent paradox that the dream commenced after it ended. The paradoxical character of the proposition is, how-

---

[1] The first question that will naturally be asked by the psychical researcher will be: Were these concurrent dreams the result of telepathy? The answer is: Possibly, but not necessarily. It is not even probable, for the reason that both were anticipating the signal gun, and the noise that caused the dreams was the same. Identical causes will always produce like effects, but not necessarily identical in detail; and it is not alleged that the two dreams were identical in detail. In order to make a case for dream telepathy there should be no common cause, antecedent or immediate. An illustrative case came within the writer's experience. The salient feature of his dream was that he saw a white-faced ox passing through a narrow lane and entering an enclosure. The dream was very vivid, but was totally void of significance, for he was not in the habit of thinking of cattle, much less of possessing any interest in them, and had not consciously had them in his mind for years. Judge of his surprise when his wife related a dream the next morning in which a white-faced ox, passing through a narrow lane and entering an enclosure, was the salient feature. There was absolutely no assignable cause, near or remote, for either dream; and yet they were both dreamed the same night; and a comparison of recollections revealed the fact that the dreams were identical, not only as to the central figure, but as to its environmental details. The triviality of the subject-matter adds to its evidential value, for it is thus removed as far as possible from causes involving anticipations, habits of thought, emotional excitation, or waking thoughts immediately antecedent.

ever, at once removed when we consider the peculiar powers and limitations of the dream intelligence, or subjective mind. As I have already pointed out, its powers of induction are nil; but its power of correct, logical deduction from suggested premises is potentially perfect. It is obvious that both suggestion and subsequent deduction are involved in this class of dreams. The sound constitutes the suggestion that a gun has been fired; and from this accepted objective fact are deduced, in their order, all its antecedent causes, near and remote; the dreamer's habits of thought in reference to guns serving to give the trend to the deductions. Thus, the sound of a cannon suggested a great battle, which was immediately in evidence. A battle suggested a state of war and incidental camp life, with its accompanying hardships. Camp life suggested antecedent drilling, from which, in turn, were deduced the rendezvous at the National Capital, the State rendezvous, the uniform, the conscription, the efforts to avoid it, the draft, etc., back to the beginning of the story. It follows that such dreams run backward; and that they are, therefore, nothing but a series of deductions from a series of suggested premises, beginning with the peripheral stimulus (auditory) which set the train in motion. It is, indeed, questionable if all dreams are not made up of series of deductions backward from the causal stimulus. The latter necessarily precedes the dream, as when the removal of the bed-clothes on a cold night causes a dream of a whole winter spent in an arctic climate. Be this as it may, it is evident that when the stimulus lasts but an instant, and begins where the dream story ends, the latter must necessarily consist of a series of deductions as stated.

The point, however, to which especial attention is invited is the inconceivable rapidity of mentation involved in dreaming a year-long dream, including an indefinite number of details, within an infinitesimal space of time. Thus, the time elapsing between the slamming of Professor Carpenter's door and his awakening to normal consciousness is inappreciable to the objective mind. Yet the dream, with all its details, was conceived within that point of time and strongly impressed upon the mind of waking consciousness. It is obvious that when the two ends of a dream are so close together in point of time, the objective mind, handicapped by its time and space limitations, could not possibly know at which end it commenced. Naturally, it interprets it in terms of its own experience, just as the mind sees objects right side up, although the images cast upon the retina of the eye are always inverted.

These wonderful powers thus found to exist inherent in the dream intelligence, together with its equally wonderful limitations, are in such marked contrast with those of normal consciousness that they constitute still further proofs of duality of mind. In fact, a complete analysis of the various classes of the phenomena of dreams would reveal ample evidence of duality, even without the aid of experimental hypnotism. With that aid it is easy to demonstrate the fact that for all practical purposes it is a safe hypothesis. Hypnotism, for present purposes, may be considered as a means of stimulating the activity of the dream intelligence, or subjective mind, testing its powers and ascertaining its limitations. In other words, hypnotism is a means by which dreams can be induced, controlled, and experimented with. It is to the human soul what the scalpel is to the human body. It is the instrument by which the soul can be dissected and its mysteries explored for the benefit of science. As the scalpel in unskilled hands may be made an instrument of destruction, so may hypnotism in the hands of ignorance or charlatanism be made the instrument of untold evil to both body and soul. In the hands of the skilled and conscientious scientist hypnotism may be, and has been, the instrument of scientific investigation of the problems of the human soul. It has rescued psychology from the domain of speculative philosophy and made it an experimental, inductive science. It has invaded the realms of superstition and destroyed the food upon which it has battened throughout all the ages of mankind. It has done this by revealing man to himself.

It found in man a living soul. It segregated it from its objective environment, mental and physical, and analyzed its powers and revealed its limitations; and, paradoxical as it may seem, it found, in both its powers and its seeming limitations. indubitable evidence of its divine origin [1] and of its immortality.[2]

All this it did — and much more — by the simple process of inducing in the subject a profound sleep, and then proceeding to experiment with that wonderful intelligence which, as we have seen, is most familiarly manifested to us in our dreams. Duality

[1] See " The Divine Pedigree of Man."
[2] See " A Scientific Demonstration of the Future Life."

was thus demonstrated by proving that the highest distinctive powers of each mind were manifested only when the powers of the other were inhibited. Besides, the fact that they are segregable at all is sufficient evidence of duality, to say nothing of the distinctive powers and limitations of each. It is, in fact, only by means of these distinctive powers that we are enabled to know that they are segregable, or when segregation has been accomplished. That is to say, were it not for the distinctive powers, one mind or state of consciousness would be a mere duplication of the other, differing, perhaps, in degrees of power, but not in kind. In that case the trance condition, spontaneous or induced, would be a mere exaltation of the objective powers, — a hyperesthesia of the physical senses. Braid, indeed, attempted to show that the phenomena of mind-reading could all be thus accounted for. But later as well as earlier experimentation demonstrated the contrary, and not only firmly established telepathy upon a scientific basis, but definitely located the power in the subjective mind.

This wonderful power, together with others not necessary to enumerate in this connection, served to differentiate the two minds or states of consciousness so clearly that duality became a hypothetical necessity. And what is true of the distinctive powers of the subjective mind may be repeated with multiplied emphasis with reference to its limitations. Of these, the one which particularly interests the student of mental therapeutics is its constant amenability to control by the subtle power of suggestion. This subject, however, must be reserved for treatment in subsequent chapters. It is sufficient for present purposes to note the fact that suggestibility, in the psychic sense, is a limitation pertaining exclusively to the subjective mind. The objective mind is hedged about by no such limitation, nor by anything remotely akin to it. It is mentioned here merely as one of the psychological discoveries of experimental hypnotism which swells the volume of evidence for duality of mind.

It is entirely safe to say that not one fact has yet been brought to light, by the psychological experts of this or any other age, that disproves, or tends to disprove, the fundamental fact of the dual character of man's mental organism. It is equally safe to aver that there is not one fact or phenomenon within the whole range of the physical sciences that disproves, or tends to disprove, the fact of duality. In one of my former works [1] I collated a series of facts showing that experimental surgery had demonstrated the fact of duality. In another work [2] I brought the undisputed and indisputable facts of organic evolution to bear upon the same subject with the same result. The discussion cannot be repeated here for obvious reasons. I can only say, in conclusion of this branch of the subject, that if the facts of psychology proper fail to convince, the facts of the physical sciences demonstrate the essential truth of my first proposition, — that man is endowed with a dual mind, objective and subjective.

[1] See "A Scientific Demonstration of the Future Life," chap. xv.
[2] See "The Divine Pedigree of Man," part i., " Evolution and Psychology."

CHAPTER V

THE LAW OF SUGGESTION (HISTORICAL)

A Law must be formulated in Terms indicating Universality before it
can be made available for Scientific Purposes. — Antagonism of
Conservative Science. — Opposition to Newton's Discovery — The
Laws of Duality of Mind and of Suggestion dimly perceived for
Ages. — The two Laws Necessary Concomitants of each other. —
The Recognition of their Relation a Prerequisite of their Formu-
lation. — Jesus the First to promulgate the Law of Mental Healing.
— His Declaration of the Therapeutic Potency of Faith confirmed
by Modern Science. — Braid's Experiments in Hypnotism. — Lié-
bault's Discovery of the Law of Suggestion. — This Law incomplete
without the Law of Dual Mind. — The Importance of the Law of
Suggestion outside the Field of Therapeutics.

IT is axiomatic that nature's laws are of comparatively little use to science, as means for the
advancement of human knowledge, until they have
been formulated. Formulation presupposes generalization, and generalization presumes universality.
This presumption, however, is subject always to
further investigation and to consequent disproof,
and it is disproved when an exceptional case is discovered; for nature's laws are immutable and
admit of no exceptions. If, therefore, it is found
not to be universal, it is not a law, and all conclusions based upon it must be revised. Nevertheless,
a universal law must be formulated in terms indicating universality before it can be made generally

available for scientific or practical uses. It may have been floating around loosely in human consciousness for ages, and it may have been found useful in specific cases by an indefinite number of individuals, and those individuals may each have formulated a law applicable to his own field of research; yet it is not universally available until some one collates the different classes of cases, and crystallizes the thought involved into a concrete form of human expression indicative of universality.

When this is once accomplished, however, — such is the "conservatism of science," or the perversity of human nature, — the discovery is generally destined to encounter three successive stages of opposition. First, it is met by a universal shout of derision. When that fails to disprove it, as it sometimes does, everybody claims it as his own. When that is disproved, as it sometimes is. each claimant proceeds to cover himself with the dust of old libraries in an effort to prove that it was always known.

Newton was not exempt from the usual course of opposition. His discovery was derided in scientific circles; he was encountered by rival claimants; volumes have been written to prove that there is no such force as the attraction of gravitation, and still others to prove that Newton did not discover "gravity," the proof being that the term had been in common use long before Newton was born. Nevertheless. no one has yet succeeded in robbing Newton of the credit of the discovery that the force which the world has consented to designate as "gravitation" acts with an energy proportioned directly as to the mass and inversely as to the square

5

of the distance; and that the formula is as applicable to the apple which falls to the earth as it is to the movements of the planets. Nor is the lustre of his name dimmed in the slightest degree by the fact that his discovery was made possible only by Kepler's previous discovery of the laws of the planetary orbits; nor by the fact that the success of his work finally depended upon Picard's correction of the old measurement of a degree of the earth's surface. All great discoveries are necessarily the resultants of all previous subsidiary discoveries.

The laws of duality and suggestion furnish striking examples of laws dimly perceived for ages, used by many, discovered in subsidiary sections, so to speak, and finally formulated as a universal law, and thus rendered available for the uses of all mankind.

The great factor in the retardation of the final establishment of the two laws consisted in the fact that they are the necessary concomitants of each other. That is to say, suggestion is necessary to duality, and duality is indispensable to suggestion. In other words, a clear conception of the law of suggestion, as it manifested itself in its protean aspects, was impossible in the absence of the theory of duality; and, on the other hand, duality was inconceivable in the absence of some salient point of differentiation between the hypothetical two minds or states of consciousness; and suggestion furnished a point of differentiation so clear and unmistakable that duality became a logical as well as a psychological necessity. Necessarily, until this concomitant interrelation of the two laws was clearly perceived, and they were formulated together as necessary parts of a psychological whole, the prevailing ideas on the subject were chaotic to the last degree.

Thus, the theory of duality has been dimly floating around in the minds of various philosophers, from the time when Greek philosophy ruled the intellectual world until the present age, without seriously affecting the trend of psychological thought. The phenomena indicating it were, of course, the same as they are now, and the theory was often tentatively advanced. But religious thought was apparently hostile to it, and the arguments of the Church were at the time considered unanswerable. Thus, John Locke,[1] in discussing the phenomena of dreams, puts into the mouth of an opponent, real or imaginary, the following paragraph, which is now known to be substantially true.

" Perhaps it will be said," says Locke, " that in a waking man the materials of the body are employed, and made use of, in thinking; and that the memory of thoughts is retained by the impressions that are made on the brain, and the traces there left after such thinking; but that in the thinking of the soul, which is not perceived in a sleeping man, there the soul thinks apart, and making no use of the organs of the body, leaves no impression on it, and consequently no memory of such thoughts."

This position Mr. Locke strenuously repudiates, declares it absurd, and proceeds with an argument against it which, in turn, cannot now be characterized by any milder term than that which he applied to the dual hypothesis.

[1] Human Understanding, vol. i. book ii. chap. i. p. 86, ed. 1884, London.

The history of the dual hypothesis, however, is of little interest or scientific importance compared with that of the slow development of the idea which culminated in the formulation of the law of suggestion.

As I pointed out in the first chapter, Jesus of Nazareth was the first to give authoritative utterance to that divine law of mental healing which it has taken science nineteen hundred years to rediscover. Jesus was not a scientist, in the modern sense of the word, and he did not attempt to teach his followers by the employment of scientific terms. He simply told them the truth in language that they could comprehend; and when he stated to them that " faith " was the mental attitude essential to successful mental healing, he epitomized in that one word the whole law of therapeutic suggestion. What is the essence of the law of suggestion? It certainly does not consist of a formula built up of words. Words are merely the vehicle of expression by which one may be made to comprehend the law. What, then, is the central idea embraced in the law of suggestion? It is simply that a certain belief, to wit, a belief in the efficacy of the particular therapeutic agency at hand, has a therapeutic potency. This is all that can be expressed in any form of words; and the word " faith," as Jesus employed it, conveyed the central idea so clearly that no one has ever mistaken its exact meaning.

Jesus expressed the same idea in different words when speaking of prayer: "Therefore I say unto you, All things whatsoever ye pray and ask for, believe that ye have received them, and ye shall have them." [1]

[1] Mark xi. 24 (R. V.).

Obviously this passage cannot be construed as referring to material benefits, for that would degrade it into a manifest absurdity; and the Master never uttered absurdities. Every word of his was pregnant with significance, and this passage is especially charged therewith. Let us analyze it.

It is self-evident, in the first place, that the blessings referred to as conditionally awaiting the suppliant must be either spiritual or therapeutic blessings, or both. They are certainly such as reach the suppliant through the mind; for their realization is distinctly conditioned upon a certain definite mental attitude on the part of the suppliant. That condition is simply *belief,* — otherwise, *faith.* The passage, therefore, is simply another way of reiterating his doctrine that faith is the one essential condition precedent to the realization of benefits that reach the individual through the mind. It is another way of saying that " the prayer of faith shall be answered." Moreover, it distinctly excludes the idea that material benefits, such as houses, lands, or money, may thus be attained through prayer; for, obviously, no attitude of mind is capable, *per se,* of producing a house and lot or a herd of cattle. It also excludes the idea of special, miraculous intervention in answer to prayer; for the conditions pertain exclusively to the mental attitude of the suppliant. But it does not exclude the implication that prayer is an effective therapeutic agent.

It must suffice to note the fact, in this connection, that Jesus evinced a clear comprehension of the central idea involved in the law of suggestion, and insistently proclaimed it on every suitable occasion.

That it was practically lost to science for more than eighteen hundred years, was due to the prevalent materialistic skepticism. That it was not wholly lost is due to the vitality of truth. The words of the Master were, in fact, never wholly lost to view, even by scientists; and the principle has often found a partial expression by scientists who sought to conceal the origin of their ideas by coining a new terminology. Thus, the " expectant attention " of Carpenter was hailed as a triumph of science, and figured largely in its vocabulary for many years, although it was a mere substitute for the word " faith," and accounted for the same phenomena. " Imagination " is another word that has performed yeoman's service in the vocabulary of science. It has been invoked, " time whereof the memory of man runneth not to the contrary," to account " scientifically " for cures effected without the use of material remedies, and then dismissed with lofty contempt, as a subject unworthy of the attention of science. Thus the French Academy, in its report on Mesmerism, admitted that marvellous cures had been effected, but learnedly attributed the result to " imagination," and thus dismissed the subject as unworthy the further attention of science. Obviously, the word was a mere substitute for that employed by the Master; and a very awkward substitute it was.

The employment of the term " suggestion," on the other hand, is not a substitution of one term for another, each being descriptive of a definite mental condition. On the contrary, it is a tacit recognition of the fact that faith is the essential condition, and the term itself is merely descriptive of the process necessary to induce that condition. As such, it was a distinct advance in psychic science, even when the law was first formulated as pertaining solely to hypnotism. Its principal value, however, consisted in that it was the beginning of the mental process by which the idea finally became crystallized into a formula expressive of a universal law. To Liébault, of Nancy, belongs the credit of taking this first distinctive step, leading to the discovery of its universality. The credit has been assigned to Braid, of Manchester, notably by Bernheim,[1] of Nancy, who was himself indebted to Liébault for all that he knew of hypnotism. It is true that the world is much indebted to Braid, first, for making hypnotism respectable by giving it a name, secondly, by inventing a new method of inducing the condition, and thirdly, by making a series of experiments illustrative of the suggestibility of hypnotized persons. But it does not seem that he did more than show that the faith requisite for successful mental healing could be induced in a patient's mind by any kind of statement, true or false, provided the hypnotic condition could be first induced. But Paracelsus made a broader discovery than that three hundred years before Braid was born; for he distinctly intimated that a false belief,[2] however induced, is just as efficacious for therapeutic purposes as a true one, — " faith " being the sole condition precedent; and Pomponazzi,[3] in the sixteenth century, gave utterance to

[1] See "Suggestive Therapeutics."
[2] See "The Law of Psychic Phenomena," pp. 147, 148.
[3] Op. cit.

expressions of identical import. Neither of these old writers, of course, knew anything of hypnotism; but they knew what Braid did not know, namely, that the therapeutic effect of faith is not limited by methods of inducing it, much less by abnormal psychical conditions.

But even after the law had been formulated by Liébault, the mystery surrounding mental therapeutics was not dispelled. It was simply shifted to another point of view without increasing the light. Up to that time hypnotism, *per se,* was supposed to be, in some mysterious way, the curative agent. When asked for an explanation of its therapeutic potency, the only reply elicited was that it was *hypnotism* that did the work. In this respect they were far behind the mesmerists, for they at least had a working hypothesis. Right or wrong, they had a theory of causation that had many facts to support it. Animal magnetism, or the theory of fluidic emanations from the healer, impinging upon the patient, had at least the merit of a valid working hypothesis. This hypothetical fluid, it was held, by its mysterious influence upon the vital principle, re-established functional harmony; and the logic of analogy was invoked in a comparison of its methods and its benefits to those of light, heat, and electricity. But " science " rejected the theory with hysterical indignation, and persistently denied the phenomena until Braid showed that he could reproduce a small part of the phenomena by processes that excluded the fluidic theory. But his master stroke consisted in giving it a new name which implied no theory of causation except that of sleep. This at once placed the whole subject upon "a scientific basis;" for not only was the name borrowed from the Greek, but it implied no theory of causation beyond what was tangible to the senses. The patients slept, and were cured, and that was all there was of it. And so it remained for about forty years, when Liébault formulated the theory of suggestion. This was resisted for a time by rival schools, but its truth was so obvious and so easily demonstrable that its opponents were at last forced to yield. This, of course, supplied a long-felt want, namely, a theory of causation for hypnotic phenomena; and again hypnotism was placed upon a "firm scientific basis."

But this, in turn, was unsatisfactory to the rigidly scientific mind and conscience. It was an explanation that did not explain. It simply removed the explanation one step farther back, and thereby deepened the mystery.

It is undeniable that in suggestion a mental *process* is found for inducing in the patient the prerequisite mental condition for healing him, namely, faith. But it is obvious that it is not the suggestion itself that does the healing, although we are frequently given to understand that it is. To read a work of the early suggestive therapeutists, one would imagine that "suggestion" was an entity that does things. Hence we are told that suggestion does this and does that; and that is all the explanation they are able to give of the science of mental healing. In other words, the rationale of suggestion is not in evidence in their working hypothesis. Nevertheless. it has done, and is still doing, a great work; and it constituted a gigantic stride in the evolution of experimental psychology as applied to mental medicine.

But, as I have already pointed out, it required the theory of the dual mind to complete the working hypothesis for mental healing. Under no other theory, or possible theory, can it be explained why a suggestion is able to induce the requisite mental condition To say that it works its results by " exciting the imagination of the patient " is to employ a phrase of indefinite meaning where an intelligent entity is indicated. A suggestion is a statement made by one intelligent being to another presumably intelligent being; otherwise it could produce no result, physical or mental. A therapeutic suggestion, in order to be effective, must be a statement addressed to an intelligence whose faith can be stimulated, and who possesses the power to carry the suggestion into effect. Such an intelligence is found in the subjective mind of man. In short, the " vital principle " of which scientists in all ages have discoursed so learnedly, is an intelligent entity, — or at least an organized intelligence, — controllable by suggestion, and invested with full power to control the vital functions.

That this is true is attested by all the facts of psychological science pertaining to the subject-matter. Not one fact of either mental or physical science militates against it. I submit, therefore, that, if true, the dual theory is another step in advance toward placing mental medicine upon a scientific basis, in that it shows *why* suggestion is an effective agency in the cure of disease.

But another step is required before suggestive

therapeutics can be truly said to be invested with the dignity of a science. It still remains to show *how* the subjective intelligence is enabled to produce its wonderful therapeutic results. Of course, this can be done only approximately, by showing that the necessary and appropriate machinery exists in all sentient organisms for that purpose. I have already hinted at the subject; but a full discussion of it must be reserved until the third term of our therapeutic formula is reached in its order.

In the meantime enough has been said to justify provisionally the broad generalization of the law of suggestion embraced in the second term of our formula, namely, that " the subjective mind is constantly amenable to control by the power of suggestion," and this without reference to the states or conditions, hypnotic or otherwise, of the objective mind.

Let me make myself clear upon this point, for its practical significance is as broad as the realm of human intelligence. Bernheim, in pursuance of the then prevailing theory limiting the scope of the law of suggestion to definite pre-existent states or conditions, defines hypnotism as " the induction of a peculiar psychical condition which *increases* the susceptibility to suggestion." [1] (The italics are mine.) He had previously noted that certain persons were susceptible of suggestion in their apparently normal state, to a more or less limited extent; and he also knew that hypnotized persons are, as a rule, more easily controlled by suggestion than they are in a normal state. Hence his apparently correct conclusion that

[1] Suggestive Therapeutics, p 15.

hypnotism merely *increases* the susceptibility to suggestion. But therein lurks a fundamental error, for it implies a limitation that does not exist. It would be more exact and truthful to define hypnotism as "the induction of a peculiar psychical condition which" *releases the subjective mind from the dominance of adverse auto-suggestions.*

The subjective mind is "constantly" controllable, and controlled, by suggestions, coming either from without or from within, the latter arising from habits of thought, or settled principles, or convictions, or prejudices, as I have pointed out in previous chapters. They are termed auto-suggestions, or self-suggestions, and they often prevail against suggestions from others. As in all other contending forces of nature, the stronger necessarily prevails. Obviously it was the lack of a clear conception of this fundamental principle that led the Liébault-Bernheim school of suggestionists to assume limitations to the law of suggestion, or, what was equally unscientific, to imagine that there can be exceptions to a law of nature.

It must be said in extenuation, however, that when they began their investigations the prevailing ideas were in a chaotic state; and further, that, for the mere purposes of practical therapeutics, the hypothesis, as they formulated it, was sufficiently near the truth to give them the machinery of suggestion to work with.

On the other hand, now that it is known to be a universal law of the subjective mind, it is at once seen that its field of usefulness is as wide as the domain of human thought; and that, of all the laws of the human soul, the law of suggestion is the most

important, so long as it inhabits the mortal body.
I have elsewhere [1] shown that amenability to suggestion is a limitation pertaining solely to this life,
and that in the future life it is no longer in evidence,
the soul being endowed with the Godlike power of
intuitive perception of all truth pertaining to its well-
being and its stage of development. I cannot repeat
the discussion here for obvious reasons. It must suffice, in this connection, to point out some of its uses
in this life outside the domain of mental therapeutics. Nor will the intelligent reader be surprised
when he is told that the law of suggestion is a factor
of equal importance in every other field of human
activity. For instance, it is the one all-important
factor in the education and development of children,
morally as well as intellectually. As in mental therapeutics, it has been ignorantly employed throughout
all the ages, and its variant effects have resulted
from the accidents of environmental conditions, and
not from a knowledge of the law itself, — in ignorance, in fact, of its existence. Nevertheless, the
law existed from the very beginning of sentient life,
and it has performed its mission as a civilizing agent
in all the variant stages of human development. As
in mental therapeutics, it is adapted to all conditions,
and performs its humanizing mission in spite of
ignorance and superstition But, again as in mental
therapeutics, certainty and permanency of results can
be achieved only when man understands the law and
intelligently applies it to its legitimate uses. When
that knowledge is attained, every mother will have
in her own hands an easy and absolutely certain

[1] See "A Scientific Demonstration of the Future Life."

means of controlling the energies of her children and directing them into whatever channels of activity she may elect. It is axiomatic that "knowledge is power," and "know thyself" is a time-honored injunction to mankind. Combining them, it may be truly said that to "know thyself" is the certain means of obtaining power and dominion over others. Without unduly anticipating what is to be said in future chapters of this book, it may be said that when the parent is armed with a knowledge of the law of suggestion he is possessed of the means, not only of directing and controlling the general education of his children, but of directing the moral trend, anticipating bad habits or curing them when formed, removing undesirable or vicious traits of character, inspiring industry and ambition, and even of removing or neutralizing the mental or moral obliquities due to heredity.

Nor are the mental and moral effects of suggestion confined to the young; for adult criminals may thus be reformed and restored to usefulness, although with less certainty of immediate results Bad habits may be eradicated in the adult, as well as in the child, by the judicious employment of suggestion. Other things being equal, the effect is the same.

Nor is this all; for good suggestions, of whatever character they may be, or to whomsoever they may be addressed, invariably react upon the character of the suggester. It is impossible for one to suggest moral principles to another without being morally benefited himself. It is impossible for one to be a drunkard when he is employing suggestion for the eradication of drinking habits in another. I have known men to be utterly unable to bear the smell or taste of liquor after making a series of strong and vigorous suggestions to a drunkard that the taste or smell of liquor would thereafter make him sick. I knew one — a moderate but habitual user of intoxicants — to be made violently ill by taking a small drink of whiskey after making such a series of suggestions to a drunkard. This occurred to him three times in succession before he divined the cause. He was an amateur suggestionist, and not well grounded in the principles of the science he was practising. Otherwise he would have known that under the law of duality an auto-suggestion is as effective as a suggestion from another. The objective mind suggests, and the subjective mind accepts and believes the suggestion and performs its functions accordingly. In other words, it takes note of the suggestion made to another as to the effect of liquor upon him, and with the inexorable deductive logic of the subjective mind, it deduces the conclusion that the taste of liquor will make anybody sick.

I have known several hypnotists who lost their former drinking capacity after treating others for the eradication of the habit. Some of them realized the reason, and some did not — which is but another way of saying that some knew less than others about the intricate workings of the law of suggestion. I have, in fact, never known one who has been able to retain his capacity to drink liquor, even moderately. after treating others for the habit of drunkenness, without a determined effort to do so, — that is to say, by resorting to a course of vigorous auto-suggestions.

It will thus be seen that auto-suggestions are as effective for the eradication of bad habits as are the suggestions of others; and I unhesitatingly affirm that any one can thus relieve himself of any habit he *sincerely desires* to get rid of. But it often happens that the patient has no real desire to be rid of his habit; and this constitutes an adverse auto-suggestion which necessarily defeats the object. The same remark applies to all suggestions for the eradication of habits, from whatever source they may emanate.

This, however, is a slight digression. The point which it is desired to enforce is that all suggestions to a patient react upon the one who makes the suggestion. As has been before remarked, action and reaction are always equal; and the principle is as true of mental as of physical energy. As the teacher is benefited by fixing the lesson taught more firmly in his own mind, so is a suggestion, moral or therapeutical, beneficial to him who makes it. Like the quality of mercy, " it is twice blessed; ·it blesseth him that gives and him that takes."

CHAPTER VI

SUGGESTION IN LOWER ANIMAL LIFE

Evidence for the Laws of Duality of Mind and of Suggestion must be found in Lower Animals. — The Subjective the Primordial Mind. — The Brain a Product of Evolution. — The Subjective the Mind of Instinct and Intuition. — Necessity for Secondary Instincts. — Induction in Lower Animals. — Secondary Instincts created by the Objective Mind. — The Mental Processes Involved. — All Evolutionary Development of Animal Intelligence due to Suggestion. — The Law of Suggestion an Essential Factor in the Progress of Civilization. — It is the One Available Means whereby Man may neutralize the Evils due to Heredity.

IF the most rigid adherent to the strictest rules of scientific, inductive investigation of the phenomena of nature were to be asked to name the kind and amount of evidence necessary to demonstrate scientifically the truth of the proposition that amenability to suggestion is a universal limitation of the subjective mind, he would doubtless reply that it must be clearly shown that the law embraces the lower animals, and that no amount of research or quality of evidence that did not include the lower animals could possibly establish so broad a generalization. no matter how strong the evidence might be that it is a universal limitation of man's subjective powers. Otherwise it might eventually be found to be a phenomenon incident alone to the environmental conditions with which man is surrounded, and not a universal law of the subjective mind. In other words, if it is a universal law of the subjective mind it must apply to all subjective minds, of whatever grade of intelligence. It follows that if it cannot be shown that animals are subject to the law of suggestion in precisely the same way that man is, the idea that it is a universal law must be abandoned. On the other hand, our most rigid scientist would admit that if it can be shown that, allowing for the difference in the grade of intelligence, the law applies to the lower animals the same as it does to the human species, it can be fairly claimed that the universality of the law of suggestion has been demonstrated as clearly as any psychological proposition is demonstrable. The same remark applies to the law of duality. In fact, since duality and suggestion are correlative propositions, as I have already pointed out, they must stand or fall together, from whatever point of view they may be considered.

The first question, then, to be determined is, What evidence exists to show duality in the mental organism of the lower animals; or, in other words, what evidence exists to show that they are endowed with the subjective mind as distinguished from the objective mind? To this the broad answer must be returned, provisionally, that all the facts of organic evolution, physical and mental, conspire to demonstrate the proposition. The scientific evolutionist will at once admit that duality in man presupposes the same in his earthly ancestors. If man is descended from the lower animals, — and no scientist now pretends to doubt the truth of that proposition, — it necessarily follows that all the salient characteristics of man's mental organism exist, in embryo, in that of his humble progenitors. Besides, it is a time-worn proposition of evolutionary science that the potentialities of manhood reside in the lowest unicellular organism.

In point of fact, the most conclusive evidence of the existence of a subjective mind — and consequently of duality — is found in the lower animals, from the moneron to man; for in tracing the ancestry of man backward to the first manifestation of life and mind in unorganized (Haeckel) protoplasm (the monera), we find that the subjective mind antedated the objective mind by untold millions of years. Haeckel tells us that during more than one half of all the millions of years that have elapsed since the beginning of organic life on this planet, no animal possessing a brain was in existence. It follows that the brain is a product of organic evolution. Like every other physical organ, it was evolved in response to a necessity,—to supply a long-felt want, to serve a purpose for which the subjective mind was not adapted. The latter is the mind of instinct in the lower animals, the mind of intuition in man, — which is a distinction without a real difference in function. The primary instincts with which it was endowed were sufficient for the ordinary purposes of animal life in its native environment; but as animals grew in number and variety, environmental conditions were constantly changing, and new or secondary instincts were required to enable the animals to adapt themselves to new environments. All biologists [1] agree that ani-

[1] See quotations from Darwin, Romanes, and others, in "The Divine Pedigree of Man," where this subject is more fully elucidated.

mals require secondary instincts, that is, new instincts, for this purpose, and that they acquire them by a definite process; that is to say, they first meet the new conditions, wants, dangers, etc. "intelligently," and after the new habits thus acquired have been practised for several generations, these habits become crystallized into instincts, and are thenceforward inherited the same as the primary instincts. It will thus be seen that they tacitly admit that there are two grades or kinds of intelligence in evidence even in the lower animals, namely, instinctive intelligence, and the other kind, which they do not name. But, as I have shown elsewhere,[1] they are hopelessly at sea as to when this new intelligence, which is thus able to cope with new environments and to educate the instinctive intelligence, came into existence, and how it performs its functions; in other words, they are hopelessly at variance as to when animals began to reason.

The dual hypothesis, however, renders a solution of these problems perfectly obvious, for we have only to refer to the facts of experience to enable us to find it. Thus, we know that the brain is the organ of the reasoning mind; that that mind alone is endowed with inductive powers, and that it is only by the exercise of these powers that we are enabled to cope with the constantly changing environmental conditions of physical life. We know that the greater our inductive powers are, the more perfectly we are armed for the "struggle for life," —which is a struggle to overcome or adapt ourselves to adverse environmental conditions; and we

[1] Op. cit.

know that in the entire absence of these powers we should be as helpless as the amœbæ. We know, therefore, that the mind of which the brain is the organ is especially adapted to the necessities of a physical life; and we infer, with unanswerable logic, that the brain, with its highly specialized powers and functions, was a product of organic evolution. Moreover, we are confirmed in this induction by the fact that it appeared at the opportune moment, — that is to say, when it became a necessity as a means of promoting the further progressive development of organic life. From that moment mere brute force ceased to be the only factor in the survival of the fittest. Induction supplanted it just in proportion to the development of that power, until in man it is the predominant factor; for it not only gives him dominion over the whole brute creation, but over the forces of nature. In other words, it enables him to create his own environment in defiance of adverse conditions.

Let me not be misunderstood in reference to the inductive powers of the lower animals. Induction is simply the process of estimating the relative and the cumulative values of facts. In its higher development it enables us to learn something of the laws of nature and to harness its forces for the uses of mankind. Its simplest processes are employed in discriminating between two or more facts, and the first brain that was developed in animal life on this planet performed that function. It was feeble, of course, but it served its purpose. for the animal with brains survived and soon dominated the organic world. Feeble as were its powers in the beginning, it was able to educate the subjective mind, and thus create or develop secondary instincts adapted to new and constantly changing environmental conditions. The result was what one would have a right to expect under the theory of the dominating influence of the objective mind; namely, the animals that possess the greatest objective intelligence are invariably endowed with the most complex instincts. All modern biologists now admit that this is a rule without a known exception.

It follows that the objective mind is the dominating factor in the mental organism of the lower animals just the same as it is in that of man, and that the vast congeries of complex secondary instincts with which men and animals are endowed originated in each case in the objective mind. How? Let Darwin answer: "Intelligent actions, after being performed during several generations, become converted into instincts and are inherited, as when birds on oceanic islands learn to avoid man."[1] Romanes extends the same principle in the following language: "Intelligent adjustments when frequently performed become automatic in the individual. and next they are inherited till they become automatic habits in the race."[2]

Darwin's reference to the birds on oceanic islands points to a very apt illustration of the principle under consideration. When the white man first made his appearance on those hitherto uninhabited islands, he found the native birds to be devoid of the fear of man. Having never seen one, they were unaware

[1] Descent of Man, p. 67 (Appletons' ed., 1896).
[2] Mental Evolution in Animals, p. 268.

that the human biped in his savage and semi-savage state is the natural enemy of all birds; but they soon learned the lesson, and they learned, moreover, that he was armed with a weapon that was fatal to birds at long distances. The result was that they soon intelligently adapted themselves to the new environmental conditions, — that is, they avoided the new danger, by making themselves exceedingly scarce in the immediate vicinity of the " man behind the gun." It is further alleged that they very soon learned to measure with great accuracy the effective range of the guns, — just as our native crows have learned to know the same thing, and, moreover, to keep pace with modern improvements in fire-arms.

It is further stated, with reference to the sea-island birds, that the generations of young birds born immediately subsequent to the advent of man were as fearless in presence of the latter as were their ancestors when man first invaded their habitat, and remained so until they were educated by the example of the older birds, or learned the lesson from their own experience. Nevertheless, after an " intelligent " avoidance of the new danger " during several generations," the fear of man was converted into an inheritable instinct, and thereafter the youngest bird was as fearful of his enemy as was his most experienced ancestor.

The question now is, What were the mental processes employed in the creation of the new instinct? Obviously the first step involved was the exercise of the powers of induction; for there were at least three facts to correlate and a conclusion to be drawn. The first fact was the man, the second was the gun, and

the third was the effective range of the gun; and the
conclusion was that within certain limits of distance,
which the bird was able to measure or estimate with
practical exactitude, the man and the gun constituted a combination that was fatal to birds. Whether
the bird was able to consider the man and the gun
as separate or separable factors in the combination,
our informant does not state. But it is well known
to every American farmer's boy that our native crow
is able to perform that inductive feat; that is to say,
he knows that the crow is provokingly fearless of
man when the latter is without a gun and correspondingly shy when the fatal combination is in evidence. Moreover, the crow is able to correlate the
three factors, — namely, the man, the gun, and a
certain definite area of territory; and he knows that
the elimination of any one of them is fatal to the
efficiency of the combination.

This is just as truly a process of induction as was
that which Newton employed in his search for the
law of gravitation: and it just as certainly involves
the collection, classification, and correlation of facts
for the purpose of arriving at a general conclusion,
as did the process which Kepler employed in his
search for his three laws of planetary motion.

Being a process of induction, it follows that it
originated in the objective mind, — the mind of
which the brain is the organ, — the mind of " intelligence," as distinguished from the mind of " instinct," — the mind whose office it is to educate
the subjective, or instinctive intelligence, and guide
it through the intricate mazes of a physical
environment.

Is there any doubt as to the scientific accuracy of the last proposition? Locke says that "God does not make noble things for ignoble uses," which is true in a limited sense. If he had said that *God does not make noble things without any uses*, he would have propounded a "universal postulate," for its opposite is inconceivable. And this is precisely what God would have done if He had created a brain intelligence capable of inductive reasoning, when there was already in existence an organized intelligence endowed with the same powers and capable, actually or potentially, of performing the same functions. It is an axiom of evolutionary science that no physical organ was ever evolved except in response to a necessity growing out of physical environmental conditions; and this is as true of the brain, with its distinctive functions and faculties, as it is of the antennæ of the humblest insect.

As I have repeatedly had occasion to observe, that which is now designated as the subjective mind exists in all sentient organisms, from the moneron to man; its salient characteristics are the same now as in the primordial epoch, varying only in degree; and its one salient limitation of power is due to what science, for want of a better name, has designated as the law of suggestion. I have also shown that comparatively late in the history of organic evolution a new mental power was developed, capable of supplying the deficiency due to the limiting law, and thus imparting a fresh impetus to progressive development in the organic world. I repeat that this new power would not have been evolved but for the necessity which existed; and hence the

specific character of the new power is demonstrative
evidence of the character of the deficiency or limitation.   Not that it imparted any new powers to the
already existent mental organism, but that it was
able intelligently to direct and promote the enlarge-
ment of the scope of the old.   I have endeavored to
point out the process by which this was begun, —
namely, by the development of new or secondary
instincts, — and that this was possible only under
the correlative laws of duality and suggestion.

I have said that no new powers were imparted to
the subjective mind; nor were its limitations removed.   Obviously that would be impossible without
changing or repealing a law of nature.   The same
limitations must always exist so long as it is hedged
about by a physical environment.

It will thus be seen, (1) that all progressive
increase of animal intelligence beyond primordial
conditions is due to the development of secondary
instincts, from time to time, in response to the necessities growing out of new and constantly changing environmental conditions; (2) that the acts of
secondary instincts are at first " intelligently " performed, and are afterward crystallized into inheritable instincts; (3) that the " intelligence " which
thus adapts itself to new environmental conditions
is primarily that of the objective, or brain, mind;
(4) that the objective mind was, and is, the in-
structor of the subjective mind; and (5) that all
progressive development of animal intelligence is due
to the suggestions of the objective mind to the subjective mind.

It follows that *all evolutionary development of*

animal intelligence is due to the law of suggestion; that is to say, all acquisitions of knowledge that are inheritable, and therefore permanent and valuable to the species, are due to that one universal law. For until animal intelligence is converted into an instinct it is not inheritable, and until it is inheritable it is not permanent, and until it is permanent it is of little value to them in the struggle for life.

What is true of the lower animals is also true of the higher animals, including man. The same law that prevails in the acquisition of the secondary instincts which enable the lower animals to cope successfully with new environmental conditions, enables man to assert and to maintain his dominion over all the animal creation,[1] to educate his children, and to train them for future usefulness in the moral and intellectual realms.

It follows that the law of suggestion is an essential factor in the evolution of civilization as well as in the evolution of animal intelligence. As such, it

[1] Were it not for the law of suggestion, it would be impossible for man to tame a tiger, subdue an elephant, or break a horse. Thus, every one is aware that in order successfully to reduce a horse to permanent subjection to the will of man, he must be made to believe that man is stronger than a horse. This is usually done by throwing the animal and holding him down until he ceases to struggle. When that has been successfully accomplished, the rest is easy; for the suggestion has thus been imparted to the limited intelligence of the horse that it is useless to struggle against superior strength. This principle prevails in all encounters between man and the lower animals; and just in proportion to man's success in imparting that suggestion to the animal he seeks to subdue, will he succeed in rendering the animal permanently obedient and docile. In a word, man is enabled to assert and maintain his dominion over the animal creation solely by virtue of the law of suggestion.

is the antithesis of the law of heredity, which has been rightly termed "the conservative factor in evolution." Heredity simply preserves what has been gained by evolution. It takes no step in advance; it accomplishes no new result. Indeed, its tendencies, under the law of atavism, are retrogressive. Evolution, with all its factors and forces, is progressive; and as suggestion is its prime factor, especially in moral and intellectual advancement, it follows, as before remarked, that suggestion is the antithesis of heredity. In this sense, therefore, suggestion may be defined as *the one means, available to man, whereby he may avoid, overcome, or neutralize the evils due to heredity.*

It is, therefore, not only the prime and all-potent factor in the evolutionary development of animal life and intelligence, but it is the one supreme psychological factor, without which human civilization would be impossible.

Enough has now been said to show that the first two terms of our hypothesis are demonstrable propositions. It remains to prove that the third term is equally veridical,—namely, that "the subjective mind controls the functions, sensations, and conditions of the body." This we may assume, for the present, to have been provisionally established by the testimony of "a cloud of witnesses," including that of the ablest members of the medical profession, to say nothing of the innumerable evidences of it in the records of cures of disease under the thousand and one systems of mental healing, generically known to science as "Suggestive Therapeutics." But it will more fully appear as we proceed with the discussion hereinafter.

CHAPTER VII

SUGGESTIONS ADVERSE TO HEALTH

The more Beneficent a Law of Nature, the Heavier the Penalty for its
Violation. — This Axiom as applicable to Laws of Life, Mind, and
Health as to any other Law. — Exemption of the Lower Animals
from Suggestions Adverse to Health. — Man the Prey of such Sug-
gestions. — The Potency of Adverse Suggestions equal to that of
Therapeutic Suggestions. — The Newspaper an Agency for the
Promulgation of Suggestions Adverse to Health. — The Patent-
Medicine Advertisement. — The Danger of Adverse Suggestions
to Students of Medicine. — Newspaper Literature relating to Diet.
— Pernicious Dietetics. — Auto-Suggestion the Safeguard.

IT is axiomatic that the more beneficent a law is,
the heavier are the penalties exacted for its violation. This is divine justice, and in the realm of
natural law the rule is inexorable. Hence the highest conception of human justice, in criminal jurisprudence, is to " make the punishment fit the crime."
Owing, however, to human imperfections, the highest
ideal is not often, if ever, reached, although it is
more and more nearly approximated as humanity
rises in the scale of civilization; hence the gradual
restriction of the death penalty to violations of the
laws for the protection of human life.

In nature's laws the inexorable rule is as above
stated; and no amount of culture or experience or
evolutionary development can enable one of God's
creatures to evade the full penalty exacted by nature

for the violation of one of her laws. Necessarily this is as true of the laws of life, mind, and health as it is of any other. If it were not, there could be no such thing as a science of psychology or of physiology or of therapeutics; for nothing could be safely predicated upon the truth of that most fundamental of all the axioms of science, — " the constancy of nature." In fact, one of the surest methods of definitely ascertaining and confirming the existence and universality of a supposed law of nature is by systematic observation of the evils resulting from its violation. This is especially true of the laws of health, as is shown by the fact that most of the important discoveries in therapeutical science were the results of observations of pathological conditions of the human body or of the mind. If the penalties are constant and uniform, coextensive with the real or supposed range or scope of the law itself, and commensurate in each case with the magnitude and character of the infractions, it is presumptive, if not conclusive, evidence of the existence of the law.

To this test we must now submit the law of suggestion. If the axiom is true that " the more beneficent a law is, the heavier are the penalties exacted for its violation," we shall have a right to expect to find that a perversion of the power of suggestion is followed by untold evils to body, mind, and soul. And this, as I shall attempt to show, is borne out by all human experience. For the present, however, I shall confine myself to the domain of therapeutics, although enough will be said to show that the principle applies with equal force to every field of human activity.

Two questions have been asked by speculative philosophers of all the ages, neither of which could ever be satisfactorily answered prior to the discovery of the law of suggestion. The first is, Why are the lower animals so much more healthy than the human race? The second is, Why does man grow weaker as he grows wiser? Both these questions have been answered more or less satisfactorily from various standpoints, but it is now safe to say that the law of suggestion reveals the prime factor in the solution of both problems.

In the first place, the lower animals, owing to their lack of intelligence, are entirely exempt from the influence of suggestions adverse to health. The same is true of idiots and of many insane persons, and for the same reason. In neither case can adverse suggestions reach the subjective mind, owing to the limited intelligence of the objective. Hence " nature," as the world loosely defines that mysterious energy within which keeps us alive, is left free and untrammelled to follow its natural trend, which is always toward health and the conservation of the vital forces.

On the other hand, man, whose objective mind is capable of receiving and assimilating impressions from innumerable sources, is the constant prey of suggestions adverse to health; and the most significant feature of it is that, the more numerous are the sources from which man receives his impressions, the greater are the dangers which beset his pathway through life. In other words, the history of the world shows that as the sources of information multiply, the diseases of mankind increase in number and prevalence; and this in spite of man's increased knowledge of medicine, sanitation, and hygiene. This fact alone points unmistakably to a psychological cause; and to those who have followed my remarks thus far it will be obvious that popular ignorance of the law of suggestion is responsible. For if suggestion is a therapeutic agency as effective and universal as we have found it to be, it follows that suggestions adverse to health must be equally potent in the other direction. This view of the case will be confirmed if we find that suggestions adverse to health are as common and as prevalent and as virulent, so to speak, as the diseases themselves. That is to say, we may expect to find that the increase of such suggestions, and the facilities for imparting them to the public, are proportioned to the increase in the number of diseases which afflict mankind; and this, as a matter of fact, is precisely what we do find. Beginning with the lower animals and idiots, neither of whom are capable of receiving either a therapeutic suggestion or one adverse to health, and ascending through all the grades of human intelligence, we find that this ratio prevails. It follows that as in these days books and newspapers furnish facilities, greater than ever before existed, for imparting suggestions to those who read them, we may expect to find that books and newspapers are the prime sources of the suggestions, good or bad, which dominate mankind of the present day. Now, it cannot be denied that the press, especially the newspaper, leads the van in the world's material and intellectual progress; but it is equally true that the newspaper, as a means of promoting or promulgating psychological knowledge, has thus far proved a dismal failure. This is not the fault of the newspaper, *per se;* but it arises from the fact that the average newspaper man shows the prevailing ignorance of the fundamental principles of psychology, especially of the new psychology. I shall not stop to dwell upon the fact that the new psychology, in the hands of ignorance, readily lends itself to the uses of newspaper sensationalism, for that is not the worst feature of the situation. It matters little that the newspaper has succeeded in frightening its readers into an insane prejudice against hypnotism, for popular prejudice against that psychological agency is not without its value in guarding the public against the possible evils of hypnotism in the hands of ignorance and charlatanism. But the case assumes a serious aspect when we consider the newspaper as an agency for the promulgation of suggestions adverse to public health: and the fact that it is done unintentionally and in ignorance of the law of suggestion serves but to enhance the gravity of the situation.

The first and most obvious agency through which the newspaper assists in the promulgation of suggestions adverse to health is the patent-medicine advertisement. Everybody is familiar with the patent-medicine man's insidious ways, and with what preternatural cunning he insinuates ideas of ill health into the minds of his readers. If his medicine is not a panacea for all the ills that flesh is heir to, he usually selects some disease that is quite common — say, dyspepsia, or liver complaint, or kidney trouble, or impure blood — and then pro-

ceeds to tell us that all other diseases arise from the
particular disease which he has selected for a base
of operations. He then proceeds to dilate upon the
fatal character of his selection, and usually appends
a long list of " symptoms " by which any one can
know that he is a victim. The list is always extensive enough to include every conceivable sensation
that is at all uncomfortable, so that few healthy persons escape, and none who are watchful for pathological "symptoms" in themselves can possibly count
their cases outside of the fatal category. Fortunately
for the patent-medicine business, the latter class is
very numerous. In fact, there are few persons who
cannot, by persistent " introspection." evoke any particular " symptom " that has been suggested. The
tendency to do so is one of the serious difficulties
encountered by the students of pathology in our
medical colleges; and before the law of suggestion
was understood by the faculties, many students were
compelled to abandon their studies because of their
irresistible tendency to " imagine," and eventually
to experience, every symptom of the diseases they
were called upon to study. Some, indeed, of the
more persistent paid the penalty of death by diseases
brought on by the suggestions borne in upon them
by their studies. I personally know one physician, a
graduate of a regular medical college, whose usefulness has often been seriously impaired in critical
cases by the fact that he almost invariably " took on
the conditions " of the patient while at the bedside,
especially if the patient experienced any great amount
of pain, — cases of parturition forming no exception
to the rule. Husbands have been known to suffer

equally with their wives in such cases, and instances are not uncommon where the husband suffers all the pangs of " morning sickness " during the pregnancy of the wife. In one case the husband was personally known to the author. His first experience occurred while he was temporarily absent from home, and it continued for two weeks before he returned. In the meantime he consulted an eminent physician who happened to be familiar with the phenomenon, having met with several such cases in the course of his practice. He recognized the symptoms at once; but the fact of the absence of the husband from home when he was first attacked puzzled him, for telepathy was not then recognized as a possible factor in such cases by physicians of the old school. Nevertheless, the doctor was so sure of the significance of the symptoms that he urged a comparison of notes when the husband returned home; " for," said he, " what mysterious bond of psychological sympathy may exist between husband and wife, no one can tell." A comparison of experiences proved the correctness of the doctor's diagnosis; for the husband's and wife's sufferings were found to have been coincident as to time and character, day by day, from the beginning.

This, however, is a slight digression. My object is to show how easily and powerfully suggestions may operate to bring about pathological conditions in people of far more than average intelligence. If medical students can be so wrought upon by the suggestions embraced in their general studies of pathology and their subsequent experiences at the bedside, what may we not expect of that large and constantly augmenting class whose knowledge of pathology is derived solely from the patent-medicine advertisements in the daily papers? This question is especially pertinent in view of the fact that a very large proportion of that class are never so happy as when they can find in themselves an illustrative example of the pathological science to be found in the patent-medicine advertisement.

Suggestions arising from this source are, however, among the very least of the evils resulting from newspaper science of medicine; for, bad as are the influences of the patent-medicine advertisement, it is not without its mitigating factors. In the first place, the medicines themselves are generally harmless; and in the second place they carry with them very potent suggestions as to their therapeutic efficacy. These are in the form of "testimonials" from those who have been "raised from the dead" by means of the nostrums advertised; and as such testimonials are usually very cheap and easy to procure, especially from those who are fired with an ambition to see their names and pictures in print, or from decayed statesmen, they are generally abundant in quantity and of a quality exactly suited to the demands of trade. Many such testimonials are, no doubt, genuine; but be that as it may, they perform the functions of a therapeutic suggestion in reference to the remedy advertised, and thus elevate the patent medicine to the standard therapeutic value of the placebo of the regular practitioner. And this is saying a great deal for the patent medicine; for the average physician is never entitled to so much confidence as when he administers a placebo accompanied by a vigorous therapeutic suggestion. In the hands of the prudent physician, who is distrustful of his own diagnosis, the placebo is of the very essence of conservatism. It conceals the ignorance of the doctor, — which is in itself a measure of great therapeutic value, — and it supplies the patient's strenuous demand for medicine. It gives the physician time to study the case, and "nature" an opportunity to do his work for him. Best of all, it does no harm; and when accompanied by an intelligent therapeutic suggestion, it often does much good. To a limited extent the harmless patent medicine, when accompanied by the "testimonial," does the same thing in the same way; and hence the remark that the patent-medicine advertisement is one of the least of the evils resulting from the medical literature of the newspaper.

If I were called upon to name the most prolific source of suggestions adverse to health, I should unhesitatingly say that it is the newspaper literature relating to diet. It is safe to say that nine-tenths of all diseases of the digestive organs, especially dyspepsia, are due primarily to the suggestions embraced in that kind of literature. The exasperating feature of it is that not one newspaper article in a hundred on that topic is written by any one who knows anything about the subject. They are generally written by boys or young ladies who are learning the trade of newspaper writers. Everybody familiar with that class of people is aware that the highest ambition of the newspaper cub is to write something that will be extensively copied by other papers; and he soon learns that anything pertaining to health in general, or diet in particular, is sure of an extensive and eager hearing. Whereupon he proceeds to guess out a long list of articles of diet that are "unhealthy," because indigestible, or innutritious. or poisonous. In order to be entirely original and startling, he generally selects one or more of the most popular articles of diet in his community, and tells his readers that they are — perhaps slowly, but "certainly surely" — sapping the foundations of their respective constitutions by indulgence in this or that particular article of diet.

One of the wise sayings of the celebrated Dr. Abernethy was that "when a man begins seriously to dissect himself, he will soon be a fit subject for the undertaker." And this is precisely what the average reader of such articles generally proceeds to do. That is to say, the next time he indulges in the article of diet inveighed against, he proceeds to institute a series of introspective observations having special reference to the behavior of his stomach in presence of that particular article of nutriment, and he is generally rewarded by finding just what he is looking for. namely, some decidedly uneasy symptoms indicative of indigestion. The next time he tries it the symptoms are more pronounced; and the third or fourth trial is generally sufficient to cause that particular dish, e. g. bread and butter, to be tabooed as utterly indigestible. Then he proceeds to lecture his family and friends on the subject of the insidious but deadly character of bread and butter; and in due time that article of food is banished from the household bill of fare

The next newspaper article attacks some other

article of diet, and with the same result, and so on through the whole bill of fare of the ordinary household; the result being one or more confirmed dyspeptics in every family. It may be thought that I am stating an extreme case. It is extreme, but very common; for this is the way dyspeptics are created in nine cases out of ten. The weakness of the stomach is often due solely to atrophy of that organ; and the atrophy is due, not to eating indigestible food, nor to habitual overtaxation of the digestive powers, but to the fact that it was not given enough to do to keep its powers at their maximum. It atrophies, precisely as any other organ of the body will atrophy, for the lack of a normal amount of exercise; and the only way to give it healthy exercise is to give it a normal amount of nutritious food to digest, always taking care to avoid those mental conditions which interfere with the normal action of the digestive organs. Strange as it may appear at first glance, the latter consideration is of the first importance; for there is no such thing in civilized countries as an indigestible article of human diet, provided the proper mental conditions are maintained. Conversely, there is no article of food that cannot be rendered indigestible by the induction of adverse mental conditions. The lesson is obvious and the remedy easy, but the discussion of it must be deferred for the moment.

Another newspaper source of suggestions adverse to health is to be found in the tendency of the journalistic humorist to fadism in the construction of the so-called newspaper joke or humorous paragraph. A single illustration of my meaning will

suffice. Many years ago some preternaturally smart
newspaper cub (an Englishman, I believe) conceived the idea of conquering fame by ridiculing the
New England custom — then almost universal —
of eating pie (pronounced " paie," in the vernacu-
lar) for dessert. The only thing connected with the
custom — or the pie — that was a legitimate subject of raillery. even from an Englishman's dietetic
standpoint, was the fact that the more luxurious of
the New England pie-eaters indulged in that luxury
three times a day. But the pie joke, feeble and
harmless as it was in its infancy. survived and was
passed around in its myriad forms, and so was the
pie, until some more than ordinarily feeble-minded
newspaper pathologist lifted up his voice and proclaimed the New England pie to be the real and
only source of all the ills that American flesh was
heir to. This, of course, was heralded far and wide
as a great and an important scientific discovery in
dietetics. and the usual process of " introspection "
began in thousands of New England homes where
pie had before been a benediction and a joy unspeak-
able three times a day, to say nothing of surrepti-
tious " pieces " between meals. The usual results
followed, and in an incredibly short space of time a
" cloud of witnesses " arose to testify against pie.
A careful watching of the " symptoms " revealed
the fact that pie was " utterly indigestible." In
vain it was pointed out that for hundreds of years
it had been eaten by all classes and under all conditions by New England people, and that no one had
discovered that pie was other than wholesome as
well as palatable and easily digested, until the news-

paper fakir happened to think about it. Once started, the hue and cry went the rounds of the " family " journals, each one seeking to outdo all the others, until pie became such an abomination in the public mind that it required an abnormal development of " nerve " to defy popular opinion so far as to order a piece of pie at a public restaurant, and if any one had the hardihood to do so he was fortunate if he escaped a serious lecture by some neighboring " reformer " on the subject of the diabolical nature of pie. Even doctors were dragged into the crusade and compelled by force of public opinion to look wise and shake their heads when a convalescing patient craved a piece of pie; and Emerson was credited by a newspaper reporter with denouncing pie as the greatest evil with which the American nation had to contend. Some doctors even went so far as to claim the credit of the discovery that pie was indigestible, and others claimed to have always known that pie was the root of all evils in the American commonwealth.

To any one familiar with the potency of suggestion, it will not seem strange that in the midst of such a crusade against a particular article of diet there should be found many whose experience amply justified the crusade; and when we reflect that in every newspaper-reading family in the United States the subject of the indigestibility of pie was a common topic of conversation at the table, it is not at all wonderful that in almost every family one or more should experience a fit of indigestion after an indulgence followed by the inevitable " introspection," or watching for the anticipated symptoms. It would, indeed, have been a miracle on a national scale if these results had not followed, and pie had not been tabooed, as a consequence, in many an otherwise well-regulated household.

In point of fact, if the crusade had been started as an experiment, pure and simple, to test the efficacy of suggestion on a large scale, no better test could have been devised. For such an experiment an absolutely wholesome, harmless, and easily digested article of diet would, for obvious reasons, furnish the crucial test of popular suggestibility; and I undertake to say that the American pie is as well adapted to the purpose as any food known to civilized mankind. In saying this, I do not include the article known as "railroad pie," which is popularly believed, not without reason, to be so constructed as to render what is not sold to the famished traveller available as ballast in railroad construction. I refer to the American pie as it was made by our New England grandmothers in *antebellum* days, — that is, before the crusade was instituted against it as an institution. Did any of the crusaders stop to analyze its contents with the view of ascertaining what it is that renders pie so very unwholesome? If so, the result has never been published. Let us, then, examine it dispassionately, with the view of determining, approximately, what proportion of suggestion has been mixed in with its other ingredients in order to render it indigestible.

The American pie, *per se,* is built up of the following materials, to wit : flour, water, lard or butter, or both, sugar, and fruit, the latter normally predominating largely as to bulk. The more epicurean tastes prevailing among the aristocratic portion of New England farmers demanded a little flavoring of nutmeg, — real nutmeg, not the nutmeg of Connecticut commerce (that being manufactured solely for the export trade, as tradition informs us).

Will some dietetic crank rise to inform us what there is among the materials themselves, or in the combination, that is unwholesome, or indigestible, or even hard to digest? Is it not, indeed, a combination devoutly to be wished for by any one of simple tastes and normal appetite? Is there anything connected with it, suggestion excepted, that could have the remotest tendency to cause it to "disagree" with the most delicate digestive apparatus? Clearly not.

It is for this reason that I have employed the crusade against pie as an illustration of the fact that when once a suggestion adverse to any wholesome article of diet or drink is turned loose upon a community, it carries with it an incalculable amount of suffering among those who are ignorant of the subtle powers of suggestion. And I have spoken of the newspaper as the means by which such suggestions are most extensively promulgated, merely as an illustration of the remark made in a former chapter, that suggestions adverse to health are numerous in a community in proportion to its facilities for the promulgation and dissemination of intelligence. It follows that so long as man rests in ignorance of the law of suggestion, the higher the grade of his civilization, the more will he suffer from suggestions adverse to his health.

If the New England pie was the only wholesome

article of diet against which a crusade has been made, these words would not have been written. But the fact is, there is scarcely anything left for one to subsist upon if he pays attention to all the current "reform" literature relating to diet. One by one the most healthful and nutritious articles of food and drink have been laid under the ban, until now it would be impossible for a hungry man to indulge in a "square meal" without violating half-a-dozen or more of some one's dietetic rules and "principles;" and could such a man, after indulgence, be induced to peruse and assimilate the current literature on the subject of what he had been eating, he would be in imminent danger of a fit of indigestion that would last him a week, perhaps a lifetime. One book would tell him that the coffee with which he had prepared his stomach for the more solid foods was a deadly poison. Another would inform him that the beefsteak, or other meats, which constituted the *pièce de résistance* of his meal, was the prime source of all the ills of the human stomach, to say nothing of its irresistible tendency to brutalize humanity and incite nations to war. The next authority would inhibit potatoes because they contain too much starch, and another would inhibit the other vegetables because they do not contain enough. One authority would tell him that he did n't eat enough salt with his food: and the next would be equally positive that salt in appreciable quantities is demoralizing to the human organism. One authority tells him that it is disastrous to drink anything during a meal, and the next dietetic savant tells him that he should deluge his stomach with hot water if he expects to eat anything with impunity. And so on through the whole bill of fare, be it great or small. I undertake to say that nothing that enters into the composition of the diet of civilized humanity has escaped denunciation by somebody, at some time, as being unfit for human food. Moreover, no such denunciation of any article of food has ever been unproductive of its legitimate results, namely, a cloud of witnesses in confirmation of the assertion. Do I hear some one say that bread, " the staff of life," must be excepted from this wholesale statement? If any one supposes that bread has escaped, he " imagines a vain thing." A few years ago an American lady — a brand " new woman " — was casting about for a " mission " in life; that is to say, she longed to " reform " somebody or something, it mattered not what, so long as it held out to her a prospect of standing at the head of a great " movement." To that end it must be something new, startling, original. She inclined to dietetics, not because she knew anything of the subject, but because she was not thus encumbered In looking over the list of foods already under the ban of the " reformer," she found nothing left but bread. It is true that bread had been foully dealt with by other iconoclasts, largely in the way of rendering it unpalatable and innutritious by making it principally of bran and other refuse material; but it was decidedly a new departure to denounce bread as the " staff of death," and so she adopted that shibboleth as the key-note of her system of dietetic reform, and, for the want of anything else to live on which had not already been proven by her predecessors to be unwholesome, she advised mankind to live on nuts.

Fortunately for the American people, they are endowed with a keen sense of the ridiculous, which decidedly limits the range of their suggestibility; and, consequently, the idea did not "take" in this country to a commercial extent. But the lady flew to England, organized a Society of Bread-Haters and Nut-Eaters, started a magazine, and wrote a book, before John Bull began to laugh.

It must not be supposed that the lady was entirely destitute of followers even in this country. On the contrary, many rose up to testify to the life-destroying potency of bread and the bland beneficence of nuts as an article of daily consumption at the family table.

It will now be seen what a vast congeries of suggestions adverse to health the American stomach is beset withal. I have spoken of the public press as being largely responsible primarily for this state of affairs. But when we reflect that what is said in books and newspapers is repeated over and over at every table at which a dietetic crank is allowed to feed, it will be seen that almost every family is more or less subjected to the infliction of such suggestions three times a day. Is it any wonder that we are known as a "nation of dyspeptics"? And is it not self-evident that heretofore cause and effect have been misplaced and misunderstood? Europeans tell us that our diet is unwholesome, and hence responsible for those ills which have come to be regarded as peculiarly American, and we are only too ready to echo the refrain; whereas the fact is that in no nation on earth is the average table so bountifully supplied with good, plain, wholesome, and nutritious food as it is in the United States. It is a common saying that the average European cook could feed a family on what is wasted in an American family of the same size. Doubtless this is true; but it must not be forgotten that it must be a European family that could thus subsist. A normal American would starve to death on the same concoction of waste materials.

No; the average American need not be ashamed or afraid of either his diet or his cuisine, — for there is absolutely nothing unwholesome in the one, nor unscientific in the other. But he should avoid the current suggestions relating to both, as he would avoid famine or a pestilence; for such suggestions as we have been considering will create a famine in the midst of abundance, and a pestilence amidst the most perfect physical environment. It is a literal fact that thousands of people in this country are perishing for the lack of proper nutriment, simply because they have allowed themselves to dwell upon the suggestions contained in current literature.

Does any one doubt the control of the mind over the vital processes? Who has not experienced a total suspension of the digestive functions upon the reception of bad news? Who has not experienced a sudden and total loss of appetite upon hearing certain disagreeable subjects discussed at the table? Who has not seen half the guests at a boarding-house table suddenly disappear when the perennial idiot known as the boarding-house wag provides himself beforehand with a long hair and pretends to pull it out of the hash? There are a few who can retain sausages on their stomachs, even the bologna, in the presence of the " humorist " who fancies that he has created an original joke by alluding to the possible constituent elements of the sausage of commerce. Fortunate indeed is the man who can hurl defiance at the joker by saying, " You can't turn my stomach." It not only indicates a healthy stomach, but the assertion itself constitutes an effective auto-suggestion which fortifies the stomach against the adverse influence of the original suggestion of " dog " in the sausage.

This leads us to the consideration of the sovereign remedy for all the manifold evils arising from the congeries of suggestions which we have been considering. Obviously the remedy is auto-suggestion: for if disease can be created by one suggestion, it follows that it can be cured by a counter suggestion. The latter may be made by one person to another, as by a mental healer to his patient: or it may be made by the patient himself, — which is known as " auto-suggestion." Other things being equal, an auto-suggestion is more potent than a suggestion from any extraneous source, for the simple reason that an auto-suggestion is generally backed by the objective convictions of the patient, whereas suggestions by another may directly contravene the patient's objective reason and experience, — not that the latter may not be effective when it is made with force and persistence, but that the former are more easily and naturally effective, either as a moral or a therapeutic agency.

One may, therefore, counteract the great bulk of

the current dietetic suggestions by the employment of just a little reason and common sense. If he feels that he must read what every crank has to say about diet and health, let him ask himself if there is any reasonable foundation for the diatribe against the particular article under treatment. and in nine cases out of ten he will find that it contravenes all reason and human experience. But the safest plan is to refrain from reading such stuff; for the tendency always is to try to verify what one reads on such subjects, especially if one is ignorant of the potency of suggestion and its tendency to create expected conditions. This is on the principle that " an ounce of prevention is worth a pound of cure." It is always easy to prevent an adverse suggestion from taking effect in the mind; and that is by not allowing it to find an entrance. To that end one should never allow himself to think. much less talk. on the subject of the wholesomeness or digestibility of the food that is set before him. The good old biblical rule is the best: " Eat what is set before you, asking no questions for conscience' sake."

Above all, having partaken of a dish, do not go away and sit down to watch for symptoms of indigestion. If one does that, he will be sure to find what he is seeking. The best rule of diet is to eat what you like to eat, in due moderation of course, and never allow the question of its digestibility to intrude itself, even in an adverse thought. Indulgence in cheerful conversation during and immediately after meals is the best conceivable " dieticall and prophylaticall receipt of wholesome caution " against acute indigestion or chronic dyspepsia. In

8

other words, keep your mind off your stomach during the process of digestion, and you will soon forget that you have a stomach. The immunity of animals and idiots from diseases of the digestive organs, many of whom eat enormously of whatever they can get, is due to the fact that they are beyond the reach of suggestions adverse to health. Some one has well said that if the current dietetic suggestions could reach the mind of an ostrich, he would soon be unable to digest a boiled potato.

CHAPTER VIII

"PURITANICAL" DIET AND MEDICINE

Asceticism of our Puritan Ancestors. — Tendency of Primitive Minds to reason by Analogy. — Influence of Asceticism on Dietetics. — The Appetite usually a Safe Guide. — Dyspepsia often caused by Suggestion. — The Principle of Asceticism in the Old Medical Practice. — Importance of the Law of suggestion in Connection with Diet and Medicine.

IN saying what I shall have to say under the above heading, it is far from my intention to cast any reflections upon the character or the religion of our Puritan ancestors. It is only in reference to some salient peculiarities that a parallel can be drawn which justifies the title to this chapter.

It was these peculiarities, growing insensibly out of an ascetic religion. that drew from Lord Macaulay the remark that the Puritans of the epoch of which he was writing " hated bear-baiting, not because it gave pain to the bear, but because it gave pleasure to the spectators." [1] That this was literally true, Macaulay then proceeds to demonstrate by documentary evidence.

Of course, this trait of character constituted no part of the religion of Puritanism, *per se;* but it is undeniable that the characteristic has been inherited by later generations to such an extent that in this country, at least, Puritanism at one time came to be

[1] History of England, vol. i. p. 154.

popularly regarded as a religion the fundamental
tenet of which was that whatever is pleasurable is
necessarily sinful. Whether this was literally true
it is aside from our purpose to inquire. But that
the acts of our Puritan ancestors often justified the
conclusion is a matter of history. It is sufficient for
our present purpose to know that the rank and file
so believed, and that their belief was justified by the
pulpit utterances of such leaders as the Mathers, the
Baxters, and their more feeble imitators. Judging
from Baxter's utterances, for instance, it would seem
that the only pleasurable emotion which he considered at all legitimate was the holy joy naturally
arising from the assurance that all other sects were
destined to suffer eternal torment in the next world.
This pleasure could not reasonably be denied the
" saints;" for, as Baxter informs us, God himself
will take infinite pleasure in the eternal torments of
the damned.[1] But all other pleasures were inhibited
as being sinful. Music, dancing, laughter, feasting,
public amusements, and all kinds of games came
under the ban; and they even sought to place limitations upon the enjoyment of parental love, as being
displeasing in the sight of a jealous God, who was
apt to kill the child whose mother's affection for her
offspring was just a little too pronounced. In short,
any pleasurable indulgence that would afford a momentary relief from the contemplation of the certainty
and imminence of death, and the gloom and dampness
of the grave, was held to be essentially wicked and
deserving of punishment by means of eternal fire.

Now, it is a singular psychological fact that when

[1] Saint's Rest, chap. vi.

a popular idea takes possession of a community in relation to one subject, it is sure to be carried over to other subjects where an analogy is supposed to exist. The human mind at a certain stage of evolutionary development is prone to seek for analogies, and on the slightest provocation the most momentous "scientific" conclusions will be drawn from supposed analogies, when in point of fact the two subjects have absolutely nothing in common. Thus, the metamorphosis of the caterpillar into the butterfly has, time out of mind, been supposed to afford a valid scientific argument in proof of the immortality of the human soul, and learned logicians have solemnly set it forth as such in text-books for the use of schools and colleges. The butterfly as a symbol of immortality is beautiful and poetical, but considered as inductive proof of the survival of the human soul after death, it is grossly illogical and unscientific. The reason is obvious: the laws governing the physical structure and metamorphosis of the butterfly are laws of the organic world, whereas the laws of the human soul are spiritual laws: and it is axiomatic that no legitimate scientific analogy exists between subjects governed by different laws. As well might one hope to solve a mathematical problem by the rules of grammar.

On the other hand, the old pagan argument against immortality is invalid for the same reason. I allude to "Averroeism," or the doctrine of "emanation and absorption," which at one time threatened to convert all Europe to paganism.[1] It was an analogical

---

[1] See "A Scientific Demonstration of the Future Life;" also Draper's "Conflict between Religion and Science."

argument of the same specious character as the one alluded to in favor of immortality, for that it sought to justify conclusions relating to a purely spiritual question by reference alone to phenomena of the material universe.

In view of this tendency of primitive minds to find analogies where none exist, it is not at all strange that in a community holding fast to the idea that in the moral and social realms whatever is pleasurable is sinful, they should also believe that in the gastronomic world whatever tastes particularly good is necessarily unwholesome, and that the efficacy of medicines is proportioned to their nastiness and the consequent amount of discomfort that can be inflicted on the patient by their administration. I do not undertake to say that this doctrine has been authoritatively formulated; but it was well stated, according to a newspaper anecdote, by a little girl whose Puritan mother had refused her a second piece of pie on the ground that it would make her sick. "Oh, mamma!" exclaimed the afflicted little maiden, "it seems as though everything in this world that is real nice is either wicked or indigestible."

This expresses the true situation in a nutshell. It is probable that no one has ever formulated the idea that food is unwholesome in proportion to its palatability, but certain it is that an incalculable number of people habitually act upon that "principle." It is equally certain that it is the outgrowth — unconscious, perhaps — of the popular puritanical idea, as before stated.

Be that as it may, the fact remains, and it must be dealt with in this connection: for it is one of the most prolific sources of suggestions adverse to health that the American people have to encounter. It is obvious that if such a rule of diet is adhered to, there must be a vast number of perfectly whole-some articles of food brought under the ban at every table where the rule prevails. Children espe-cially are made to suffer by being deprived, wholly or in part, of those things which every healthy normal stomach craves. Besides, the constant sug-gestions imparted to children in regard to the in-digestibility of everything that they are fond of inevitably weakens their digestive powers, and many are thus converted into chronic dyspeptics before their milk teeth are shed.

Now, there are certain things that may be more effectively used as illustrations of what is meant, because of a radical change in popular opinion in relation to them within a few years. For instance, half a century ago watermelons were under the ban, and were consequently partaken of with great cau-tion and many misgivings as to their digestibility. Nobody could offer a plausible explanation why a watermelon contained the seeds of disease, and yet the fact remained that numerous cases of cholera morbus were traced to indulgence in that luxury. Children were especially cautioned against eating all they wanted of it, and solemn warnings of the wrath to come accompanied every little piece that was doled out. Of course, vigorous introspection followed every indulgence, and everybody who ate watermelon in the evening went to bed with his mind prepared for a wrestle with cholera morbus before morning. That the legitimate result of the suggestion frequently followed, goes without saying. A notable exception must be made in favor of the nocturnal small-boy who gorged himself to repletion upon stolen watermelons. He was immune, for nobody was present to suggest the deadly character of the fruit, and he had something to think about besides watching for symptoms of approaching dissolution. He only knew that watermelon tasted good, and he was not up in the then current dietetic science which proscribed watermelon for that very reason.

Fortunately for the watermelon trade, as well as for the health of the community, it was discovered some years ago that there is absolutely nothing in the constituent elements of watermelon to justify its bad reputation. The celebrated Dr. Tanner was the first to call public attention to the fact. He had analyzed it and found nothing in it more deadly than a little sugar mixed with a large proportion of water. He experimented with it, and found that it was more easily digested than any other known product of the soil, and hence he chose it as the very best and safest means of breaking his celebrated forty days' fast. On that occasion he simply gorged himself with watermelon, pure and simple, to the consternation of the attending physicians and the horror of the general public. But as the result justified the doctor's prognosis, the watermelon scored a signal triumph, and in due course of time it ceased its diabolical work, and now everybody eats it with impunity. The suggestion has been removed.

Hard-boiled eggs is another very popular article of diet that was for many years under the ban, evi-

dently for no other reason than because every child
likes hard-boiled eggs better than he does the half-
cooked, mussy, soft-boiled egg. That being the
case, of course he must be deprived of it, on the
usual ground; or if one is reluctantly given to him,
he is duly and solemnly informed that it will make
him sick. This state of affairs continued for centuries, and it is even now in evidence among the
more ignorant families. But the prejudice has been
gradually dying out since doctors began to prescribe
hard-boiled eggs as a highly nutritious and easily
digested article of diet for dyspeptics. They argue
that cooking food until it is palatable does not render
it indigestible. On the contrary, the palatability of
food is one of the first essentials to its digestibility,
for the reason that it increases the secretion of saliva
and the gastric juices. In fact, it may be set down
as a general rule, that, other things being equal, and
the element of suggestion eliminated, the more palatable a food is, the easier it is digested and assimilated. Hence it is that "what is one man's meat is
another man's poison." — which is but another way
of saying that not all digestive organs are alike.
That which is easy for one person to digest is difficult for another; but as a rule the one who likes a
particular article is the one who can digest it, and
vice versa. In fact, it may be set down as a dietetic
axiom that *what the unperverted stomach craves it
can digest*. By "unperverted stomach" I mean one
whose powers have not been destroyed by suggestion
or other abuses.

Of course, this is the exact opposite to the "puritanical" rule of which we have been speaking. But

physicians are rapidly coming to the conclusion that the human stomach craves most that which it most needs, and that one's appetite is a pretty safe guide to a healthful diet. That is to say, the subjective mind instinctively knows the needs of the physical organism, and it makes its wants known to the objective consciousness by appropriate stimuli. Thus, in the presence of the needed food, and often by thinking of it, the salivary glands are stimulated to action, and thus the first prerequisite to good digestion is provided in an increased flow of saliva. The stomach itself is stimulated to action by the same means, and a consequent secretion of the gastric juices is induced, thus rendering the process of digestion easy and pleasurable. It follows that the opposite course will produce opposite results, and digestion of food that the stomach rejects, or does not crave, is correspondingly slow and difficult.

Hence it is that the intelligent physician of the present time is seemingly careless of his patient's diet, and generally tells him to eat what he likes. If he restricts the diet at all, it is generally because the patient seems to expect it, and perhaps would be unfavorably impressed if the doctor failed to make a showing of wisdom in that way. In such cases the average doctor will inhibit something that he does not happen to like himself; and each one seems to have his pet aversion. I knew a doctor in Washington whose *bête noir* was boiled cabbage, and he invariably told his patients that they could eat anything they liked except boiled cabbage. " Boiled cabbage," he would oracularly set forth, " is absolutely indigestible, even by a well man, to say noth-

ing of one whose stomach is weakened by disease."
Of course the majority of his patients knew by experience that for any one who likes it boiled cabbage is perfectly easy to digest, and that it is a
staple article of diet for thousands whose stomachs
have never revealed their existence by any sensation
except that of hunger; but they soon learned that
the doctor would wax hysterical if they ventured to
defend boiled cabbage against his indictment. Other
doctors have their pet aversions which they exploit
in a similar way, but there are few left who venture
to adhere to the old rule that whatever a patient
likes must, for that reason alone, be inhibited.

Half a century ago the latter rule prevailed largely
among the medical profession in this country. Of
those who can remember so far back, few can forget
the affectionate, insinuating solicitude with which the
average doctor and the nurse would urge a convalescing patient to try to think of something that he
would like to eat. And no one will forget the fact
that when some article was named, the doctor would
invariably shake his head, look preternaturally wise,
and totally and inexorably inhibit that particular
article as being hurtful, indigestible, and otherwise
altogether unsuited to the patient's condition at that
particular stage of his disease or of his convalescence. After securing a full list of articles that the
patient thought he could relish, he would be informed
that disease had so vitiated his appetite that he necessarily craved only those articles of diet that were injurious to him in his then condition; and the homily
would end by the prescription of some " sick dish "
that the patient had already been fed on *ad nauseam,*

— and it was generally some tasteless, innutritious mess that would turn the stomach of a hungry dog.

Many cases of chronic dyspepsia were traceable to this practice; and the worst of it was that the results often seemed to justify the practice. Thus, a physician would strenuously inhibit a favorite dish merely because the patient liked it and wanted it. The inhibition would be accompanied by the usual homily on the indigestibility of that particular article, and the patient would often be warned to be very careful about indulging too freely in it even after his health was restored. The suggestion would naturally take effect; and it frequently happened that the patient could never afterward indulge with impunity in his favorite dish. Nor did it matter how harmless the article might be. I knew a boy once who during convalescence was urged to tell what he would relish most in the way of food, and in reply named a certain variety of apples of which he was particularly fond. Of course he could not have that particular variety, and he was asked to name another. But he would have his favorite or none; whereupon he was told that he could have any other variety in the orchard, but that that particular apple was extremely hard to digest, and that indulgence in it would most likely cause a relapse. He was, of course, forced to forego his desires, and was in the end fed on that which he most abominated. He managed to survive and fully regained his health; but when he came to indulge in his favorite variety of apples he found that they invariably gave him a fit of indigestion. The suggestion had taken effect. That it was suggestion, pure and simple, and that it was the one enforced upon him on the occasion referred to, is evidenced by the fact that no other variety of apples had that effect upon his digestive apparatus. That the suggestions made at the same time in regard to other foods did not have the same effect upon him, was doubtless due to the fact that he had not especially craved anything but the apples, and hence the inhibition of other things had not so surprised and annoyed him. But when he was told that his favorite variety of apples was, alone of all others, indigestible, his surprise and annoyance were complete, and the impression was lasting. Be that as it may, certain it is that no other article of diet troubled him; and many years afterward, when he came to a knowledge of the law of suggestion, he was enabled to " throw off the spell " by a vigorous course of auto-suggestion, and he thus restored the Rambo to the list of digestible fruits.

But many victims of dietetic suggestions made on that principle during convalescence were not so fortunate; for thousands have suffered all their subsequent lives from having such suggestions enforced upon them in regard to the most simple and wholesome articles of diet. Most of them believe that their sickness was responsible for their subsequent stomach troubles, and they wonder why it is that their former favorite foods have ceased to be digestible, little realizing that it was *because* it was their favorite food that the doctor inhibited it during convalescence.

Happily, as before intimated, there are but few dietetic cranks of the kind left among the doctors, and the patient is now generally left to choose his own diet, except in certain cases where solid foods are dangerous, as in typhoid fever. But many victims of the old practice still survive to make themselves and their families miserable by nursing the delusion that " whatever is real nice is either wicked or indigestible."

It was not, however, alone in regard to diet that the doctors of the early part of the last century practised upon the principle that whatever was gratifying to the patient must, for that reason, be inhibited. Thus, it was long held as a cardinal principle of practice in cases of fever that the patient must be kept in a close, warm room, and on no account be allowed to drink cold water, or even to indulge in thoughts of snow or ice. Why? No one was ever able to give any better reason than that fresh air, cold water. or ice would have given comfort and pleasure to the patient. If forced to attempt a philosophical explanation of the " system," it would be said that, " being sick, the patient's tastes are vitiated. the whole order of nature is reversed, and he necessarily craves only that which is hurtful." Of course the explanation was as idiotic as the practice was abominable; but it revealed its origin in the then prevalent puritanical idea that in the moral realm whatever is pleasurable is necessarily sinful.

Other illustrations might be given of the practice, for they were numerous, but these must suffice. I have mentioned this one because it was typical; and no one who suffered from a fever in the olden time, and survived the treatment, will fail to verify what I have said. Happily, most of the old doctors who practised under the system are dead, and physicians of the present day have reversed the practice. A fever patient is now given the benefit of all the fresh air available; he is allowed to drink all the cold water he wants; chopped ice is placed within his reach, and he is treated to cold ablutions at stated intervals. The result is that fever is no longer an unmitigated torture, and even typhoid fever is largely shorn of its ancient horrors. " Good nursing " is now the salient feature of treatment of that disease, and good nursing consists in doing everything to give the patient comfort by mitigating the severity of the fever. Under the old *régime* a good typhoid-fever nurse was one who would, with grim determination, refuse the appeals of the patient for some mitigation of the torture and cram a hideous mixture down her throat at frequent intervals.

Again, the popular idea of medicine was derived from the same puritanical source. Hence it was that the efficiency of medicine was measured by its nastiness. No medicine that was pleasant to the taste was considered of any therapeutic value whatever. The old Thomsonian, or Botanical, system of medicine was apparently devised with special reference to that " principle." At any rate, it fell on fruitful soil, for it made its appearance at the supreme psychological moment when the value of all things was measured by the one standard. If there was any other standard of therapeutic value than that of nastiness in the Thomsonian *materia medica*, it certainly was not manifest to the taste. In that system the relative therapeutic values of its different medicines were indicated by numerals; and No. 1 stood for that supreme herbal abomination known to botanists as *lobelia inflata*. If that herb had been selected to stand at the head of the list solely because of its nasty taste, no better selection could have been made. But it *was* selected because no human stomach could endure its presence for five minutes if the victim had sufficient vitality left to throw it off. In other words, it was used solely as an emetic; and an emetic was always "indicated" under the Thomsonian system, no matter what the disease might be. That the patient, if he survived, invariably felt better after recovering from the effects of a lobelia emetic, goes without saying; for it would be impossible for him to feel worse than when that particular variety of emetic was performing its mission. There are, in fact, more reasons than one why he should feel better after such an ordeal. In the first place, he feels both glad and surprised to find himself alive; and as the discomforts of illness are comparative, a lobelia emetic causes all other human miseries to seem pleasurable. Moreover, if he survives, he is encouraged, for his doctor is then enabled to pronounce a favorable prognosis. Such an abounding vitality was equal to any emergency. This, in point of fact, was the secret of the undeniable success which attended the Thomsonian system of practice in its early days. In addition to the universal nastiness of its decoctions, it required each patient to go through a certain definite "course of medicine," in which the lobelia emetic, followed by steaming and sweating, was the never-failing initiatory torture. If his vitality was equal to the strain, well and good; if not, his death was charged up to Divine Providence, or to the doctor having been called too late, or to the "'Pothecary doctors" previously in charge of the case.

This, however, is a slight digression. My principal object in writing this chapter and the one preceding it is to show what an infinite variety of suggestions adverse to health are current in every civilized community; my ultimate object being to impress upon the mind of the reader the importance of studying the law of suggestion in its relations to that most important of the affairs of every-day life, — the diet upon which he feeds himself and those dependent upon him.

No one needs to be told of the prepotent influence upon his health of the food he eats, nor does any one need to be informed that the benefit which one derives from food depends upon his powers of digestion and assimilation: but the majority of people do need to be informed that their powers of digestion and assimilation are absolutely within their own control. This is, indeed, the most important fact connected with the science of mental medicine: and when it is once generally understood, appreciated, and intelligently acted upon, the science of healing disease by any process, mental or material, will be found to be of comparatively little importance.

CHAPTER IX

AUTO-SUGGESTION

The Fundamental Psychological Principles restated. — Fatal Potency of Fear in Epidemics. — Pathological Power of "Expectant Attention." — Appendicitis. — Any Disease that can be induced by Suggestion can be avoided by Counter-Suggestion or by ignoring Adverse Suggestion. — Avoidance of Adverse Suggestion. — Suggestion in Connection with Habitual Drunkenness and Dipsomania. — Counter-Suggestion as a Prophylactic. — Danger of Injudicious Sympathy — False Dietetic Suggestions to Children.

THE reader will now once more recall the fundamental psychological propositions upon which the science of mental medicine is based. They are:—

1. That man is endowed with a dual mental organism, or mind, — objective and subjective.

2. The subjective mind is constantly amenable to control by the power of suggestion.

3. The subjective mind controls the functions, sensations, and conditions of the body.

At the risk of undue repetition, I again call attention to the obvious fact that if these propositions are true, man possesses within his own organism the means and the power to control disease, with or without aid from extraneous sources.

I have now at some length discussed, *seriatim,* the above propositions with the object of impressing their exact truth upon the mind of the student, to the end that when he undertakes to apply them to

practical uses he may *know* that he is wholly within
the realm of scientific truth, and not groping in the
darkness of mediæval mysticism or savage superstition. In other words, I desire to inspire the mind
of the student with that perfect faith which alone
is born of a knowledge of scientific truth, as distinguished from the faith inspired by authority invested
with mystery and occultism. Such was the faith of
Jesus of Nazareth. He was endowed with a perfect *knowledge* of the laws of the human soul and
of its power over the material universe, and he knew
how to direct its energies in the healing of the diseases of the body. This was the secret of his transcendent power,—of his never-failing success where
the conditions could be commanded in the patient.
He could not teach the science of mental therapeutics
to his disciples, for they were mentally unprepared
to receive or assimilate it. Their faith, therefore,
was dependent alone upon the words and the example of the Master; and hence the frequent fluc-
tuations of their power, even in his presence.

It may be that science will never be able to impart
a knowledge of the law of mental healing in such
perfection as Jesus possessed it; but in view of his
promises, may we not reasonably hope to attain a
knowledge sufficient for the practical purposes of
life.

It is in this hope that I have endeavored to point
out what I conceive to be at least a valid working
hypothesis for mental medicine. To that end I have
discussed inductively the three fundamental propositions, with what success the reader must judge. I
have also pointed out some of the sources of danger

arising from popular ignorance of the law of suggestion. I have dwelt upon the innumerable suggestions adverse to health which constantly beset the
people of civilized countries, and pointed out some
of their sources. I have laid particular stress upon
those suggestions which attack the digestive organs,
because they are the most common and easily recognized, and, on the whole, the most important. Obviously, whatever impairs our powers of digestion
and assimilation saps the citadel of our material
power. But in dwelling upon that particular source
of popular danger from suggestion, it must not be
inferred that other diseases are excluded. On the
contrary, it is well known that there is no disease
of the human body that may not be created, or simulated, by the power of mind when stimulated by
suggestion. It is asserted by physicians of experience that in cholera epidemics a large proportion
— more than half — of the cases are the result of
" fear," otherwise suggestion. There is nothing to
distinguish such cases from those of true Asiatic
cholera, except, perhaps, the absence of the true
cholera germ, or bacillus, in the suggestive cases.
It is certain that all the salient symptoms of true
cholera are present in that which is induced by suggestion, and that the percentage of fatal cases is
greater in the latter class of cases.

Again, it is well known that almost any one
can cause an increased flow of blood to any part
or organ of the body by merely concentrating his
attention upon the part. If this can be done experimentally, it follows that persistence in such concentration will eventually induce congestion, especially

if the concentration is prompted by fear of disease of the organ. It follows that no organ of the human body is immune from that prolific cause of disease.

I know that I shall be trespassing upon the domain of a popular surgical fad when I venture to instance *appendicitis* as a possible example of a disease caused by " expectant attention " or suggestion. Certain it is that in the good old days, before it was generally known that man had such a thing as a vermiform appendix concealed about his person, cases of appendicitis were very rare: and when one did come to light it was invariably said to be due to the presence of some foreign substance, — generally a seed of some fruit that the patient had eaten. But since it was discovered that the vermiform appendix can be removed for a few hundred dollars without necessarily killing the patient out of hand, the people have been educated in respect to that mysterious portion of their anatomy; and cases of appendicitis have multiplied proportionately, so that now it must be a very ignorant man (or a very poor one) who cannot manage to have at least one case of appendicitis; and no surgeon can properly be considered up to date who has been unable to capture at least half-a-dozen vermiform appendices.

I am not unmindful that surgeons are provided with a very plausible explanation of this phenomenal increase of cases of appendicitis within the last quarter of a century. They explain it on the ground that there are really no more cases of appendicitis now than formerly, in proportion to the population, but that, owing to ignorance, the doctors formerly attributed such cases to other causes, such as peritonitis, and thus sacrificed many lives that might have been saved by an operation, had the seat of the disease been recognized.

Candor compels the admission that there may be much truth in the explanation. But it certainly does not account for all the increase, nor does it explain certain salient peculiarities of modern appendicitis. For instance, formerly that disease was always attributed to the presence of some irritant foreign substance in the mouth of the appendix; now, in more than half of the cases, no foreign substance is found. But, in all reported cases, serious inflammation was found to exist, — enough, at least, to confirm the doctor's diagnosis and justify the operation. What the unreported cases reveal there is no means of knowing.

One of the salient peculiarities of the modern variety of appendicitis is that it prevails most among the educated, refined, and well to do. It seems to avoid carefully the homes of poverty and ignorance. I have no statistics to verify this statement, and it may be all wrong. But it is popularly believed to be true that " appendicitis is the rich man's disease." I certainly have never known of a case that contradicts that belief.

But it would be grossly unjust to the medical profession to accept the popular explanation of the fact, which is, of course, that the doctor's diagnosis is governed by the ability of the patient to pay for an operation. This is not only palpably unjust, but it is unnecessary In fact, if there was no other explanation, I should doubt the fact, " for they are all honorable men." To those who have followed what has been said in regard to the potency of suggestion, it will be apparent that the prevalence of the disease among the educated classes is just what one might expect, for the following reasons: —

In the first place, it is only the educated classes who know much about the disease, and it requires some knowledge of anatomy to locate definitely the vermiform appendix. The essential conditions necessary to enable one to concentrate his mind upon that appendage are, therefore, present with the well informed and entirely absent in the minds of the ignorant. That is to say, one must know where to expect pain before he can induce it by "expectant attention." The ignorant, however, are not always immune, provided they think they know where to look for untoward symptoms, and are cursed with a morbid suggestibility. For instance, I knew one of that class who once became excited on the subject of appendicitis, and proceeded to inquire of a friend just where the vermiform appendix might be found. His friend, knowing his proneness to experience the symptoms of every disease he happened to read about, purposely misinformed him by giving him to understand that it was located on the left side of the lower abdomen. As usual, he began to watch for symptoms; and, as usual, he was soon rewarded by feeling a decided uneasiness in the locality named. In less than a week he felt compelled to appeal to a specialist for relief, — which was instantly afforded, both as to his mind and his body, by being informed that he had selected the wrong locality for a good case of appendicitis. Nevertheless, it required the application of hot fomentations to relieve the inflammation that had actually been induced in the suggested location. It is needless to say that if he had been correctly informed by his friend, the surgeon would not have been defrauded of a genuine case.

Again, appendicitis is such a formidable proposition, so distressing while it lasts, and its cure fraught with such danger to life, that it naturally excites the utmost dread in the minds of those who are familiar with the current literature on the subject. It would, therefore, constitute an exception to all known diseases if it failed to be attended with the usual results due to morbid suggestibility. The class thus afflicted, after reading up on the subject, begin by being very careful not to swallow any more fruit seeds; and if one accidentally slips down, they immediately begin to concentrate their minds upon their insides. The slightest symptom of uneasiness in the proper locality is magnified a thousand fold, vigilance is redoubled and intensified, and the consequent pain and inflammation is induced. The result is an operation, revealing a case of appendicitis minus a tangible cause. The expected seed, or other irritant, is not in evidence.

Another exciting cause of morbid suggestibility on this subject is the mystery with which science — or the want of it — has invested the vermiform appendix. Scientists tell us that it is the vestigial remains of some organ that is no longer useful, whatever it may have been to our remote ancestors. This may be true; but the idea seems analogous to other assertions of science which are obviously made to conceal ignorance. Thus, scientists are prone to deny the existence of all occult things that they cannot explain, as in psychic phenomena. But the vermiform appendix is a tangible reality the existence of which cannot be denied: and inasmuch as they are ignorant of its uses, they declare it to be useless. In other words, according to the theory of science, nature made a mistake in creating it, — a mistake all the more flagrant and inexcusable in that this "functionless organ" (Gray) was placed, not where it would do the most good, but where it is a constant menace to life.

If nature were in the habit of making mechanical mistakes in the construction of vital organs, the *appendix vermiformis* might be charged up to that source: but, as no other organ has been found to be functionless, it must be presumed that God is wiser than man, — wiser, if possible, than the scientists who can find no other than professional uses for the vermiform appendix, — and that in the fulness of time that organ will be able to find a valid excuse for existing. In the meantime it will continue to be constantly enhancing in value as a source of revenue for surgeons, so long. at least, as the public remains in ignorance of the potency of suggestions adverse to health.

It is obvious that the remarks made in regard to cholera and appendicitis apply with equal force and pertinency to hundreds of other prevailing diseases, as well as to those diseases of the digestive organs mentioned in preceding chapters. The lesson is obvious, and it applies to all alike. It is that —

Any disease that can be induced by suggestion can be avoided either by a counter suggestion or by ignoring the adverse suggestion.

This is the most important lesson that any school of mental medicine has to teach, and it is but a practical expression of the old aphorism that "an ounce of prevention is worth a pound of cure." Moreover, it is a lesson that any one can put into instant practice and reap an immediate reward. The science of mental healing is, indeed, important; but it requires more or less training and experience, whereas the ability to avoid disease by mental processes is within easy reach of all sane persons who understand the fundamental principles, or the salient facts, of the law of suggestion.

The following self-evident propositions will make my meaning clear : —

1. The efficacy of mental medicine is dependent upon mental conditions.

2. Mental healing is accomplished by the induction of favoring mental conditions in the patient.

3. The one prepotent means of inducing that mental condition is suggestion.

4. The power or energy that is capable of inducing a mental condition favorable to healing disease is capable of preventing disease by the same process.

5. The power that is equal to the task of either preventing or healing disease by mental processes is necessarily equal to the production of disease, conditions being reversed.

6. Suggestion, therefore, is the one prepotent mental energy which is capable of inducing, preventing, or healing disease.

It follows that suggestion is of practical value to man in exact proportion to the uses which he makes of it. That is to say, he may make it a blessing or a curse according to the uses for which it is employed. But use it he must, for it pervades the mental atmosphere as the sunlight of heaven pervades the solar system. He cannot escape it, for it is one of nature's all-pervasive forces and knows no variableness nor shadow of turning. Like every other law of nature, it is primarily for the highest benefit of mankind; but, like every other beneficent energy, it may destroy him if, either through ignorance or perversity, he fails to place himself in harmony with it.

It is a maxim of criminal jurisprudence that "ignorance of the law excuseth no man"; yet courts and juries sometimes exercise a discretionary clemency in cases where it is clear that no wrong was intended. But nature is inexorable in the exaction of the fullest penalties for the violation of her laws, whether through perversity or ignorance; and as I have before remarked, the more beneficent the law, the more severe are the penalties for its violation.

I have pointed out the fact that in this country popular ignorance of the law of suggestion has made us a nation of dyspeptics, multiplied the rate of mortality in epidemic diseases, and virtually created a new surgical disease, painful to the last degree, fatal if not cured, and dangerous in the extreme in the process of cure; and yet I have covered only a small part of the field where ignorance of the law, and false suggestions, are doing their fatal work. I have done this, not as an alarmist, not for the purpose of advertising and promoting the sale of a new-fangled patent nostrum. — not even for the purpose of advocating a new system of healing disease. In Part II. of this book I shall point out what I conceive to be the most rational method of practising the art of mental healing. But thus far I have devoted my energies to the task of familiarizing the public mind with the fundamental law the violation of which entails disease everywhere, to the end that I might point out a remedy, without money and without price. and within the reach of all, whereby the great bulk of current diseases may be avoided, and doctors and their medicines relegated to a state of innocuous desuetude.

Those who have followed my remarks thus far have already anticipated the substance of the few words of advice with which I propose to close this part of my work.

There are two ways of avoiding the effects of current suggestions adverse to health: the first is by avoiding the suggestions themselves; and the second is by opposing a counter self-suggestion. The first is the easier and more effective: but it applies principally to those whose health is not already impaired by adverse suggestions or other influences.

What is here meant by avoiding adverse suggestions is that one should avoid reading, talking, or thinking about pathological conditions of the human body. This may seem like an advocacy of popular ignorance of those subjects; and in a sense it is such. But it is justified on the ground that the health of the masses is of greater importance than popular education in pathology. Besides, the inhibition does not exclude a proper amount of popular education in anatomy and physiology. But the study of disease should be restricted to those who expect to engage in the practice of the art of healing the sick. In this connection the reader will not forget what has been said of the proneness of medical students, and even of some doctors, to evoke in themselves, by unconscious auto-suggestion, the symptoms of every disease they are called upon to study.

My remarks, however, are not intended to apply to the acquisition of a truly scientific knowledge of pathology, whatever the object may be; but it is hoped that they may serve as a warning, even to medical students, against the practice of "introspection" with the view of finding symptoms corresponding with those they are studying. What I do strongly advise against is the common practice of reading, studying, and inwardly digesting the popular literature on the subjects of disease, and especially of diet. I have already stated my reasons at some length, and it is unnecessary to repeat beyond reminding the reader that the current stuff on those subjects is generally written by those who know least about them, — often by cranks who are themselves the victims of false suggestions by other cranks, and they of others, and so on *ad infinitum.* We have already seen how a false suggestion, based upon a false premise, perpetuates itself from generation to generation and spreads itself over new domains which are entirely foreign to the original,—as from religion to diet and from diet to medicine, etc.

Horace Greeley once remarked that "the way to resume specie payments is to resume." In like manner the lesson we are seeking to enforce may be summarized: The way to avoid suggestions adverse to health is to avoid them. That is to say, never allow them to enter your mind from any avoidable source; and if they have been thrust upon you by others, avoid dwelling upon them in your meditations. Above all, do not make a personal application to yourself of everything you chance to hear about the food that others have found by personal experience to be hurtful, for the chances are a thousand to one that they are themselves simply the victims of false suggestions. In other words, avoid "introspection" while eating and during the process of digestion; for you will surely find what you are looking for, especially if you are *expecting* symptoms of indigestion.

Again, as you value the well-being of your family and friends, do not obtrude your own ideas, if you have any, about the unwholesomeness of particular dishes on the bill of fare before you. Remember that others have rights which ought to be indefeasible, among which is the right to the undisturbed enjoyment of the pleasures of the table and the consequent good digestion. But if you are an average dietetic crank, this advice will go unheeded; for that ubiquitous personality enjoys nothing at the table except making his own infirmities conspicuous and warning others of the wrath to come if they indulge in anything fit to eat. It is a fact, confirmed by extensive observation, that one such crank, turned loose upon a perfectly healthy family, with digestive organs previously unimpaired, will gradually inoculate the whole family with his mental virus, and cause the most healthful articles of food, one by one, to be banished from the table as indigestible.

The exercise of just a little common sense will enable you to avert the consequences of such suggestions when they are thrust upon you at the table by some crank whose flow of eloquence you do not feel at liberty to restrain. All one needs to do, in most cases, is to ask oneself what reason is found in common experience, or in the inherent character of the food itself, for pronouncing it indigestible or otherwise hurtful. If none is found, he is provided with a counter suggestion based upon reason and experience, and it is his own fault if he allows the false suggestion, which contravenes reason and experience, to obtain the mastery. But if, on the other hand, he is not endowed with common sense, or, in other words, if he belongs to the class of "chronic reformers," he will be apt to accept the false suggestion for the very reason that it condemns the habits and contravenes the experience of mankind. "Whatever is, is wrong" being their shibboleth, they condemn every existing institution, custom, or habit found in civilization; and hence they inveigh against the common diet of civilized mankind with the same emotional enthusiasm that they would manifest in a crusade against the institution of human slavery. In point of fact, the chronic reformer is a factor that must be reckoned with, in more ways than one, when dealing with suggestions adverse to health and the good order of society, for he is as apt to attack the practice of monogamy as of polygamy; and even when he institutes a crusade against the recognized evils of society, he frequently does more harm than good. He not only brings his cause into disrepute by intemperate zeal and idiotic methods, as in the "hatchet crusade" for the reformation of drunkards, but the average temperance fanatic is full of suggestions that have a direct tendency to encourage drunkenness. Thus, the drunkard is constantly told that he is such because it is "impossible for him to resist" the temptation to drink when he feels like it, that it is impossible for him to reform so long as liquor is for sale, and that it is impossible for him to resist the temptation to abuse his family when he is drunk. These suggestions are so persistently iterated and reiterated and drummed into the ears of the " poor drunkards," that nine-tenths of them actually believe them, and hence regard themselves as helpless victims to be pitied and coddled, rather than as criminals deserving the lash. The result is that they do not try to resist, because the suggestion is with them that it is impossible.

The most potent suggestion, however, that the drunkard is beset withal, is the one that tells him that when he has taken one drink it is impossible for him to refrain from taking a second, and a third, and so on, until he is in a condition that renders it necessary for him to go home and pound his wife. The reason is not far to seek.

It is well known to psychologists that drunkards, especially of the class now referred to. are thrown into the subjective condition by drinking anything intoxicating. This is true of most people; but it is especially true of those who are in the habit of drinking to excess, and in many cases one glass is sufficient to induce the subjective condition to such an extent as to render them extremely amenable to suggestion. It follows that when one of that class has taken one drink, the ever-present suggestion that he cannot refrain from taking another, exerts its full influence upon him; and the result is that he does not try to resist the temptation to plunge into a prolonged debauch. When remonstrated with after the debauch is ended, he invariably says that after taking the first drink he is moved by an uncontrollable impulse to take another, after which he loses all desire to restrain himself.

This indicates the purely subjective origin of the impulse, and distinguishes it from the ordinary desire for stimulants arising from nervous or mental depression. Its subjective origin is further indicated by the fact that the impulse amounts to a positive mania, and hence it is designated as " dipsomania," to distinguish it from ordinary habitual drunkenness. Like other manias, it is a mental disease arising from some form of suggestion; and the only obvious form of suggestion that could produce the result would be such as I have indicated. It is true that it may be partly traditional; but at any rate it is kept alive and potent by the constantly reiterated declaration by temperance extremists that the " poor drunkard," having once tasted liquor, is powerless to restrain himself from continuing the debauch. It not only confirms the dipsomaniac in his infirmity, but it has a constant tendency to convert the ordinary habitual drunkard into a victim of that most appalling and dangerous of all forms of inebriety.

This may seem like a digression; but it is justified by its importance, as showing that a prolific source of suggestions adverse to health, as well as to the good order of society, is found in the fanatics and degenerates who infest every civilized community. Nothing is too sacred to be meddled with by the hysterical imbecile who holds that whatever is, is wrong.

The distinguishing characteristic of a normal manhood is the ability to adapt oneself to his environment. Individually the crank is known by his inability to live in harmony with any of his environmental conditions, religious, political, or sociological. Collectively they are recognized by their propensity to organize themselves into societies for the promulgation of "new ideas," especially such as are either incapable of verification or are palpably out of harmony with established truth. As one values a healthful mental environment, he should avoid them as he would a pestilence.

Truth perpetuates itself by virtue of its own inherent vitality, and it organizes its own following from among those who recognize it by its harmony with all other truth. It needs no human organization to promulgate it, for it is self-generating; nor to perpetuate it, for it is eternal. Every truth is itself a part of an organized system, which is coextensive with the universe of God. Hence no truth is unimportant or insignificant, for the grand system would be incomplete without it. Suspend one law of physical nature but for one moment, and the physical universe would disintegrate. Suspend one law of mind and soul, and mental chaos would supervene. And as all the laws of nature are interrelated, and constitute one stupendous unitary system, it follows that a suspension of one law, physical or mental, would result in universal chaos.

Analogous to the suspension of a natural law is its violation, for in either case the harmony of the universe is disturbed. The results differ only in that, in the case of the violation of law, the inharmony affects only the guilty party and his dependents. But as to them, the appropriate penalties are inflicted with inexorable exactitude in proportion to the extent to which the law is violated. Evil, therefore, is but another name for inharmony, and its origin is found in the violation of the laws of God, physical, mental, or moral. The laws themselves are not evil, nor are they productive of evil. From the greatest to the least, they are designed for the ultimate good of man, provided only that he places himself in harmony with them. They are the embodiment of Eternal Truth, and no false conclusion or suggestion can be derived from a knowledge of their provisions.

On the other hand, every falsehood, every error, every wrong idea is a prolific source of possible evil, for no correct conclusion can be drawn from a false premise. Hence the suggestions arising from error and falsehood are necessarily wrong, misleading, and productive of untold evil consequences; and hence the necessity for constantly guarding the portals of the subjective mind against them. The safest sentinel to put on guard for that purpose is Reason, and the price of safety is eternal vigilance.

This brings us to a consideration of the second method of averting the consequences of the current suggestions adverse to health. This method, as before stated, consists in the interposition of a countervailing suggestion, whenever an adverse suggestion is thrust upon you. The method is simple to the last degree. and it is as effective as it is easy of application It consists in denying the truth of the adverse suggestion. By this I do not mean that an open controversy should be indulged in. On the contrary, that should be avoided: for it would merely cause a reiteration of the suggestion with increased emphasis and a fresh eruption of persuasive eloquence. The denial should be made mentally, and it should be persisted in as long as the suggestion continues to be inflicted. After that the subject should be ignored, — banished from the mind.

A good way to silence a chronic dyspeptic is to boast of your own good digestive powers. It may be impolite; and certainly nothing so deeply offends a chronic dyspeptic as to be told that somebody else is immune from that malady. But self-preservation is the first law of nature. You owe it to yourself to shield your own mental and physical organism from the virus that is poisoning his; and the assertion that your digestive powers are perfect is the surest way to make them perfect, or to keep them so. It is a countervailing auto-suggestion which you owe to yourself, even at the risk of enraging your friend, the chronic dyspeptic.

Chronic invalids of all kinds are prone to discourse exhaustively on the subject of their miseries whenever they can victimize a sympathetic listener. Their egotism is unbounded: and it never occurs to them that the full history of their aches, their pains, their symptoms, and their movements may not possess the same absorbing interest to others that it does to themselves. Nor does it occur to them that they are inflicting a positive wrong upon their listeners by filling their minds with suggestions adverse to their own health. Sympathy is the boon they crave, and it is all too often injudiciously extended to them; for the sympathetic remarks of friends often amount to suggestions that confirm and increase the morbid mental condition of the sufferer.

For instance, the most dangerous blessing that a chronic dyspeptic can have about him is a sympathetic wife who is ignorant of the law of suggestion. Her constant watchfulness over his diet is something appalling. Knowing his infirmity, and dreading his erratic temper when he is stricken with a fit of indigestion, she conscientiously arms herself with all the current misinformation on the subject of dietetics, and proceeds to make his life miserable at mealtimes by doling it out as occasion seems to require. With true wifely devotion she watches every mouthful that he attempts to regale himself withal, and pounces upon him at intervals with, " Henry, you must not eat " this, or that, or the other; " it will surely make you sick." And if Henry heeds her admonitions, he makes his meal of bran bread, or, perhaps, of some other equally innutritious " mush " that is advertised in the newspapers as being " predigested." The result is that he rises from the table with his digestive apparatus still further weakened by disuse, atrophied for the want of exercise, confirmed in its vicious habits by a fresh instalment of pernicious suggestions, — suggestions made by the best of wives with the best intentions. His whole body becomes weakened for the lack of proper nutriment, and he becomes an easy prey to every disease that prevails in his vicinage. He becomes morbid in mind as well as in body. He dwells upon his infirmities in his meditations, and, in pursuit of sympathy, thrusts them upon the attention of all with whom he comes in contact. If he gets the coveted sympathy, he is confirmed in his morbidity. If not, he " gets mad," and complains that the whole world is in league against him; and if any one, in self-defence, presumes to mention his own good health, he is immediately catalogued as an enemy who is seeking to destroy the only comfort and consolation derivable from dyspepsia.

On the other hand, the hypothetical " Henry " sometimes rebels against his wife's sympathetic espionage. Weak for the lack of nourishment, he comes to the table with an enormous appetite, and proceeds to eat what he likes best, regardless of the apprehensions of his faithful wife and monitor. But he does not escape her admonitions; for she is sure to remind him that his stomach is diseased and his appetite morbid,—craving "only that which is indigestible," and so on to the end of the dismal chapter. But Henry is defiant, and, prompted by both appetite and perversity, overloads his stomach. Then follows a season of reflection upon the suggestions that have been made, self-condemnation for having eaten anything at all, and the usual introspection — watching for untoward symptoms — which he is sure to experience. If he is in business, he goes in search of his employees, and —

" Discharges the best of 'em,
  Swears at the rest of 'em,
  Kicks the office cat,
  Jumps upon his hat," [1]

and otherwise disports himself with an eye single to conquering comfort and consolation by making everybody else as miserable as he is himself. All of this might have been averted by a little judicious withholding of wifely sympathy, especially at mealtimes.

The only safe rule, either for dyspeptics or well persons, is to taboo rigidly the subject of dietetics as a topic of conversation at mealtimes. Incalculable injury is often inflicted upon the children of healthy households by the incessant watchfulness of parents over their diet, especially in regard to desserts or other luxuries of which they are particularly fond. A due amount of caution is, of course, necessary; but it should be exercised when ordering the bill of fare, and it generally is. No sane person puts a dish before his children that is hurtful. But to hear the average parent discourse to his children upon the hurtfulness of the food set before them, one would think that the cook was suspected of having resolved to poison the whole family.

The truth is that nine-tenths of the talk to children about the hurtfulness of food is prompted by motives of economy. It is a constipation of the pocket-book, rather than the hurtfulness of food, that causes many a child to be tortured by the presence of luxuries that he is not permitted to enjoy in common with the older members of the family.

[1] Holmes, " The Dyspeptic."

But whatever the motive may be, the point is that *the luxuries of the table should never be denied to children on the ground that they are hurtful.*

In the first place. if they are actually hurtful. they should not be on the table. If not, a double wrong is perpetrated against the child. To say nothing of the heartless selfishness involved in depriving a child, from motives of sordid stinginess. of his share of the good things on the table, the example set before him of falsehood and deceit on the part of the parents is a moral wrong that may affect the child's whole future. If he does not follow their example. he will at least despise his parents for setting it. Be that as it may, the outrage upon his physical organism is sure to be followed by its legitimate consequences, namely, a disordered stomach and weakened powers of digestion.

The seeds of the disease which has distinguished us as " a nation of dyspeptics " are sown in the minds of our children at the table by the incessant nagging of ignorant or sordid parents.

Nor is the wrong thus inflicted upon the little ones measured alone by the false suggestions and their inevitable consequences. The appetite of the average child is not only a good measure of its digestive powers, but its " longings " are the best evidences of what it needs. For instance, many children are possessed of what the average mother regards as a " morbid appetite " for sweets; and sweets are, consequently, inhibited, with the inevitable suggestions regarding the hurtfulness of good things in general and sweet things in particular. Of course, the more strictly sweets are inhibited the more intense are the child's longings for them. This the mother usually regards as natural perversity, inherited from our grandmother Eve, and she redoubles her vigilance accordingly.

Now, the truth is that children have an appetite for sugar because they need sugar, — because of a deficiency in the physical organism of the element which saccharine matter in some form alone supplies. "Nature" cries out for it with an insistence proportioned to its necessities, just as it cries out for water when the supply of that element is deficient.

The obvious lesson is that when a child develops a strong appetite for sweets, instead of filling its mind with false suggestions as to the hurtfulness of what it craves, it should be given free and unlimited access to the sugar-bowl. Nothing is more nutritious than sugar, and few things are more easily digested and assimilated. As in case of all other nutritious foods, a strong appetite for it is good evidence, not only that the system needs it, but that the stomach can digest it, — provided always that the functions of that organ are not interfered with by adverse suggestions.

Suggestions apart, few children who have a strong appetite for sugar have ever been injured by giving it to them in practically unlimited quantities. On the other hand, many such have been grievously injured by being deprived of it; and I have known weakly, puny children to be rendered strong and robust by satisfying what appeared to the mother to be a morbid craving for sugar.

The remarks made about sugar apply with somewhat diminishing force, perhaps, to foods of which sugar is a prominent ingredient; for example, the ordinary sweet-cakes and other desserts in common use on American tables. Few, if any, are so compounded as to justify withholding them from children who are fond of them.

It is not my province, however, in a work like this, to lay down any hard and fast rules of diet. This is not a cook-book, nor is it a treatise on dietetics. My duty will have been performed to the best of my ability when I point out the salient features of typical cases where false and pernicious suggestions do their deadly work. In other words, I can only point out general principles and invite attention to a few illustrative examples. In carrying the principles into practice everything must necessarily be left to private judgment; and I can only enjoin upon my readers the necessity of exercising just a little common sense, remembering that there are but a few simple rules to observe in the employment of suggestion as a prophylactic, or preventive of disease. The most important are the following: —

1. Avoid all suggestions, from extraneous sources, which are adverse to health.

2. If such suggestions are forced upon you, meet them by counter suggestions affirmative of your own immunity from the suggested diseases.

3. Inhibit all conversation at the table adverse to the quality of the food set before you, especially as to its supposed indigestibility.

4. Never refuse to give a child the food it desires *on the ground* of its hurtfulness. If you are too stingy to give him what he wants, say so. But, as you value the health of your child, never suggest that

the food he eats is liable to "make him sick,"—first, because you know you are lying, and, secondly, because he will find it out some day, and despise you for it.

5. Talk hopefully to the chronic invalid, for his sake; and for your own sake, when you leave him, thank God that you are immune from his diseases.

6. Think health and talk health on all suitable occasions, remembering that under the law of suggestion health may be made contagious as well as disease.

7. Finally, meet the first symptom of disease with a vigorous and persistent auto-suggestion of your immunity from disease or of your ability to throw it off. When you go to bed at night, direct your subjective mind to employ itself during your sleep in restoring normal conditions, strongly affirming its ability to do so; and when you rise in the morning, assume the attitude, in mind and body,[1] of restored

---

[1] The significance of this remark will be better understood when it is known that in hypnotic experiments it has been found that the attitude of the body reacts upon the subjective mind, producing corresponding suggestions of the most powerful character. Thus, the placing of a hypnotized subject in a devotional attitude induces corresponding feelings, which in turn are carried over into corresponding actions and expressions; whilst placing the subject in a pugilistic attitude and doubling his fists, enrages him and induces corresponding actions, often of the most pronounced character. By reasoning from these well-known facts, the conclusion was deduced that a powerful therapeutic auto-suggestion could be made by assuming the bodily attitude of strength and vigor, for example, standing erect, throwing the shoulders back, expanding the chest, etc., accompanying the action with a corresponding mental attitude and words affirmative of renewed vigor and immunity from disease.

I am indebted for this idea to one of the ablest of Ohio jurists, who has for many years given much intelligent attention to the study of

health and vigor. Should these prophylactic efforts fail to produce the desired effect, and should disease come upon you in spite of them, it is not the fault of the system. It is because you are not well grounded in the conditions precedent to success. Mental remedies are dependent for success upon mental conditions, just as physical remedies are dependent for their efficacy upon physical conditions.

Obviously, the necessary mental conditions cannot always be commanded in the adult who has been reared in an atmosphere of doubt and incredulity regarding the efficacy of other than material remedies. Faith in the latter has been crystallized into a race prejudice which has been enhanced by the gross superstitions and obvious charlatanry of many who practise mental therapeutics. It will take years, perhaps centuries, to overcome the evil thus wrought.

Again, there are many who fail through persistent perversity, or, to put the most charitable construction upon their conduct, through sheer weakness of intellect, — inability to comprehend the simplest proposition relating to the conditions of success in suggestive therapeutics. Nothing can induce them to assume a hopeful, or even a passive, attitude of mind. They take special delight in being able to say that they

---

suggestive therapeutics, especially to auto-suggestion as a prophylactic agent He informs me that he has derived untold benefit from the practice; and my own subsequent observations and experience confirm every word that he says. Extreme weariness, bodily or mental, may be relieved in that way, thus enabling one, in cases of emergency, temporarily to renew his activity. Deep inhalations of atmospheric air are valuable accompaniments to the practice, as they revitalize the blood, promote its circulation, and stimulate to normal activity every cell of which the body is composed.

have not been benefited in the least by the treatment, even when it is a palpable falsehood. In a word, no argument can induce them to refrain from continually making auto-suggestions adverse not only to their own health, but to the possibility of its restoration by other than material remedies.

Obviously, suggestive treatment, in the ordinary sense of the word, is not adapted to such cases. It must be a "larvated suggestion" (Pitzer), if any, that can overcome either the perversity or the imbecility thus manifested.

To such, and to all who from any cause fail to experience the benefits of suggestive treatment, my advice is to go at once to the physician in whom they have the most confidence, without reference to the school to which he belongs. It is far more important that you should have confidence in your physician than it is that he should know anything about your case; for in the latter event he will doubtless give you a placebo, which is always safe, and usually efficacious when administered with its due proportion of suggestion. This is what Dr. Pitzer designates as a "larvated suggestion." It is in common use among the medical profession, and its value as a therapeutic agent cannot be overestimated.

Part Two

THE CORRELATION OF THE FACTS OF
PSYCHOLOGY AND PHYSIOLOGY IN CONNECTION
WITH MENTAL HEALING

Part Two

THE CORRELATION OF THE FACTS OF PSYCHOLOGY AND PHYSIOLOGY IN CONNECTION WITH MENTAL HEALING

———

CHAPTER I

INTRODUCTORY

The Facts of Psychology and Physiology to be Correlated — All Organic Tissue composed of Intelligent Microscopic Cells. — Disease of the Body is Disease of the Cells of the Body. — The Cells amenable to Control by the Subjective Mind. — The Fluidic Theory of Mesmerism. — The Nancy School. — The Force or Energy which controls the Bodily Functions a Mental Energy. — It operates upon the Subordinate Intelligent Cells through the Nerves. — Histionic Suggestion. — The Nerves the Mechanism for the Conveyance of Therapeutic Impulse from Healer to Patient. — Histionic Suggestion effective without Hypnotism and in Defiance of Adverse Auto-Suggestions.

CONSIDERED from a purely psychological standpoint, the working hypothesis for mental healing which is set forth in Part I. of this book seems to be complete and valid; that is to say, it fully and completely explains all the facts of purely mental healing that have yet been brought to light through the indefinite number of "systems" that are now in vogue or of which history informs us.

Much remains to be done, however, before mental medicine can be said to rest upon a purely scientific basis. Other sciences remain to be explored, namely, physiology and histology, or physiological psychology, before an adequate knowledge of the subject can be approximated; for, whilst the force or energy employed in mental healing may be purely psychological, that energy is expended upon a physiological structure. This presupposes a nexus between the two; and although this nexus may be intangible and hence incapable of being dragged to light by means of the surgeon's forceps, we may hope to find the machinery in the anatomical or histological structure of man, through which the psychological energy operates in the production of therapeutic results. If, then, we find the mechanism especially adapted to its supposed uses. a great point will be gained, for we shall have a right to infer that it is so employed. In other words, the correlation of the facts of psychology with those of physiology with reference to the problem of mental healing will afford conclusive evidence as to the correctness of our fundamental psychological hypothesis. Moreover, as the discovery of a new truth invariably leads to a solution of old problems, it is hoped that this will constitute no exception to the rule.

I hope, therefore, to be able, first, to point out the physiological machinery through which the subjective mind operates to produce therapeutic results. In this there will be nothing new to science except my conclusions; for I shall accept, at their full value, all the facts which modern science has discovered in reference to the histological structure of sentient beings, — facts which no scientist pretends to doubt or deny, — facts which lie at the basis of all accepted modern physiological science. To this end I shall draw largely upon the accepted facts of histology, which is the branch of biology that treats of the structure of the tissues of organized bodies, — in short, microscopic anatomy. The salient histological fact upon which I shall dwell is that all organic tissue is made up of microscopic cells, each one of which is a living, intelligent entity. This includes the bones, hair, and nails, as well as the muscles and nerves, and all other portions of the organic structure.

I shall also accept the latest and most universally accepted, because the most obviously true, theory of disease; namely, that a disease of the body is a disease of the cells of the body. This is, indeed, a corollary of the demonstrable fact that all organic tissue is composed of cells. It follows that the cure of disease consists in restoring the diseased cells to normal health and activity (metabolism). How to effect that object, however, is where doctors disagree.

Thus far my statements will not be disputed by any living scientist, or by modern doctors of medicine who keep pace with the discoveries of medical research. But when I attempt to show that the cellular structure of the physical man is the basic fact of mental healing, I shall probably run counter to some very old and very pronounced prejudices. Nevertheless, I shall attempt to show that these intelligent entities, which we call cells, and of which the whole body is composed, are obviously amenable to control by mental impulses from the central intelligence which controls the functions of the body, and that they, in fact, constitute the machinery by and through which the mind controls the body in health and disease. Nor shall I be entirely unsupported in this view, for I shall be able to quote the highest materialistic authority admitting the existence of a central intelligence in man which controls the functions of each individual cell of which the whole body is composed. In fact, no intelligent person denies the existence and potency of this central power and intelligence which keeps the machinery of **organic life in opera-**tion. It has been variously designated as " the vital principle," " the principle of life," " the soul," " the communal soul," " the unconscious mind," " the sub-conscious mind," " the subliminal consciousness." " the subjective mind," etc., the designation being governed by the point of view from which the subject is treated. But no one, be he materialist or spiritualist.[1] denies its existence. or that it is endowed with an intelligence commensurate with the functions it performs in organic life. Philosophers may differ in their views as to its origin, or its ultimate destiny, or its psychological significance outside of the functions it performs in keeping the machinery of life in motion; but no one denies its existence, its intelligence, or its power over the functions, sensations, and conditions of the body.

It will be seen, therefore, that I am not citing any facts that are new to science. I am merely giving a slightly new interpretation to the old and universally admitted facts of science when I point out the obvi-

---

[1] I use the word in its broad signification, as the antithesis of "materialist."

ous truth that this central intelligence, operating upon the myriad intelligences of which the physical organism is composed, constitutes the mechanism, so to speak, by which the mind controls the body in health and disease.

I have ventured to designate this central intelligence as the " subjective mind;" and I have shown, in Part 1. of this book, that it is constantly amenable to control by the power of suggestion, — thus pointing out a means by which the machinery of mental healing may be set in motion, either by the patient himself or by others. In doing so, however, I have merely reiterated, with the greater emphasis and elaboration that are justified by added years of experience and observation, what I had previously laid down in " The Law of Psychic Phenomena." In that work I was the first to formulate a working hypothesis, applicable alike to all methods, for the systematic study and practice of mental healing; and I am proud to say that since then many successful schools of suggestive therapeutics have been founded whose faculties acknowledge that formula to be the expression of the fundamental law of mental medicine. And I hasten to remark that, in what I shall have to say hereinafter, nothing of that formula will be taken back or modified; but much will be said in explanation of phenomena that have hitherto, in the opinion of many, refused to range themselves under the law of suggestion.

I allude especially to the phenomena of so-called " animal magnetism," or, as it has been designated in honor of its supposed discoverer, " mesmerism." This includes all those seemingly miraculous cures which, in both ancient and modern times, have been effected by personal contact or digital manipulation, — otherwise, " the laying on of hands."

It is a matter of history that in all the ages of mankind marvelous cures have been effected by the laying on of hands. But no attempt was ever made to account for the phenomena on anything like scientific grounds until Mesmer essayed an explanation on the hypothesis of fluidic emanations from the healer, impinging upon the patient, and carrying with them a fresh stock of health and vitality. The logical absurdity of explaining the unknown by something still more unknown seems never to have occurred to either Mesmer or his followers: and they made the all too common mistake of taking it for granted that when once a name was given to a phenomenon, all further explanations were superfluous and impertinent. And so it happened that Mesmer's followers held, and still hold, with hysterical insistence, that the term " animal magnetism " affords a complete scientific explanation of the phenomena of healing by laying on of hands, passes. or other forms of digital manipulation. If asked what " animal magnetism " is, they reply that it is a " fluidic emanation " from the healer; and if pressed for an explanation as to what the " fluid " is, their reply is that it is " animal magnetism " And there you are, — forever in the " vicious circle."

In the meantime the scientific opponents of Mesmer have been equally loud and insistent and hysterical in their opposition to the fluidic theory, even when constrained to admit the phenomena, — which most of them denied for many years. But none of them has ever yet offered a valid reason for denying either the phenomena or the fluid. It is a popular belief among them that Braid utterly disproved the fluidic theory by his peculiar methods of inducing hypnosis. But Braid never claimed that he had done more than to prove that *some* of the phenomena of mesmerism could be produced without the personal contact of the operator with his subject. On the other hand, he acknowledged his inability to produce the higher phenomena of mesmerism by his processes, and contented himself with casting aspersions upon the genuineness of such phenomena as he could not reproduce or understand. I refer particularly to the phenomena of telepathy or thought-transference, which were at that time being constantly produced by the methods of mesmerism or animal magnetism, — that is, by personal contact.

In later times the opponents of the fluidic theory derived much comfort from the discovery of the law of suggestion. Following the lead of the Nancy school of hypnotism. they ascribed every effect to the suggestions necessarily embraced in making mesmeric passes, when they were made for avowedly therapeutic purposes. And in all candor it must be admitted that such passes, when made with avowed curative intent, constitute a very powerful suggestion, and one which might succeed independently of any other factor in the case. But when it is known that young children — too young to understand the import of any form of suggestion — and even animals, according to the authority of the early mesmerists, have been cured by mesmeric or magnetic manipulation, it will be seen that there is something in their

processes that cannot be accounted for on the theory
of suggestion, as that term is at present understood.
In point of fact it must be admitted that the fluidic
theory was vastly strengthened by the fact mentioned;
and if there was no other way to account for the
facts, I should be slow to dogmatize against the
fluidic theory, absurd as it appears in statement and
in the absence of other than negative evidence to
support it.

It seems to me, however, that we have not far
to look for a valid working hypothesis when we stop
to consider what is known to science of the character of the mechanism through which the subjective
mind operates to control the functions of the body.
Let us, then, make a brief provisional examination
of that mechanism, reserving our proofs of each
proposition for subsequent chapters.

We may start with a universal postulate, which
requires no proofs, and which will not be disputed,
namely, —

1. The force or energy which controls the bodily
functions from within is a mental energy.

This proposition, obviously true as it is, seems to
have been overlooked by those who deny the power of
mind over the body in health and disease. It embraces, in fact, the very gist and essence of mental
medicine; for the initial impulse which stimulates
and controls the functions of each and every cell of
the body is necessarily a mental impulse proceeding
from a central intelligence.

2. This central intelligence necessarily operates,
through appropriate mechanism, upon the subordinate intelligences.

3. The subordinate intelligences are the cells of which the whole body is composed, each of which is an intelligent entity, endowed with powers commensurate with its functions.

4. The means of communicating intelligence both to and from the central, controlling mental organism are the nerves, which are composed of highly differentiated cells whose intelligence, like that of every other group of cells, is especially adapted to the functions which they perform.

5. The nerves of each organ of the body have peripheral termini, — one in the back near the spinal column, and the other in front, (approximately) near the location of the organ.

6. The nerve terminals in the cuticle are composed of still more highly differentiated cells which are especially adapted to the performance of two functions, — namely, experiencing the sensations of pain or of pleasure, and (especially those in the tips of the fingers) of communicating with, or taking cognizance of, things extraneous to the bodily organism (sense of touch). These are the most highly differentiated cells in the whole periphery of the body.

Thus far the crassest materialism will not venture a denial of my propositions; for they embrace the facts which science has discovered and promulgated in standard works, without reference to their bearing upon the question which we are now discussing. Nor will any scientist deny that the central intelligence which controls the bodily functions, by whatever name it may be designated, is amply provided with facilities for exercising its powers; that is to say,

it is in possession of the mechanism through which
it can convey to every cell in the body the necessary
mental stimulus to regulate its functions.   Nor will
any educated physician doubt or deny the proposition
that this central intelligence is susceptible of control
by the power of suggestion.

But that question is apart from my present purpose,
having been already discussed at some length.   What
I now wish to inquire is, What light does the examination of the bodily mechanism throw upon the question of so-called magnetic or mesmeric cures, or, what
may be generically known as curing by " the laying
on of hands," — the oldest. the most generally practised, and withal the most effective of all the ancient systems of mental medicine?   Is it a " fluid
emanation" from the healer — fluid health, fluid
vitality — segregated from a reservoir of fluid health
existing in the healer and impinging upon and
flowing into the patient?   Or is it a mental therapeutic impulse conveyed from the subjective mind
of the healer to the affected cells of the patient, by
means of cellular rapport established by personal
contact, through the mechanism which we have been
describing?

I have no hesitation in declaring my firm con-
viction that the latter is the true explanation of all
the marvellous phenomena which, in all the ages,
have followed the laying on of hands for therapeutic purposes.   Considered merely as a working
hypothesis, it embraces all the essentials of validity,
for it accounts for all the facts, — which is more
than can be said of any fluidic or magnetic theory,
from that of Mesmer down to the vague speculations

of the humblest of his followers. Moreover, it does not seek to explain the unknown by reference to a hypothetical something still more unknown. On the contrary, it correlates the known facts of physiological science which are pertinent to the question, with the known psychological facts bearing upon the case, as I shall attempt to show more clearly when I come to discuss the subject in greater detail.

In the meantime I hasten to say that the acceptance of this hypothesis does not necessitate a revision of the fundamental law of mental medicine as stated in the first part of this book. It merely reveals the existence and potency of a hitherto unknown or misunderstood form of suggestion. I have ventured to designate it as *Histionic* [1] *Suggestion,* for the obvious reason that it is conveyed through the cellular tissues of both healer and patient. It is, of course, a mental impulse, rapport being established by digital contact, —otherwise "the laying on of hands,"—the peripheral cells of the two thus impinging and forming a continuous chain through which a mental therapeutic impulse can be conveyed. The intelligent reader will at once correlate this with the well-known facts of thought-transference by means of personal contact, which is sometimes called "muscle-reading," to dis-

---

[1] "Histionic" is a word not found in any English dictionary with which I am acquainted. It is employed by Professor Haeckel in his "Riddle of the Universe" in connection with "histology;" and partly to avoid coining a word, and partly for the sake of euphony, I have adopted it. Derived from the same Greek root as "histology," the science of organic tissues, it appropriately designates a form of suggestion that is conveyed by a mental impulse through the cell intelligences of which the body is composed.

tinguish it from " telepathy," which is mind-reading at a distance.

It will thus be seen that the same physiological mechanism that is employed by the subjective mind to convey a mental therapeutic impulse to a diseased organ from within may be employed by another subjective mind from without for the same purpose. The mechanism is there, — the telegraphic line is open, its terminals are available because they extend to the periphery, and pain proclaims, in unmistakable language, the point where the outside connection is to be made. It is as simple and obvious as the connecting of two telegraphic instruments by joining their wires. The instruments, being identical in construction, vibrate in harmony the moment the connection is established, and intelligence may be conveyed from one to the other. The essential condition is that the wires must be joined. And so it is with the human instrumentalities They are identical in structure in all essential particulars. Each individual is possessed of the mechanism for communicating intelligence; and the condition essential to communication with each other is that their " wires " shall be connected. The wires of the human instruments are the nerves; the connection is made by bringing the nerve terminals into contact, and this is done by the laying on of hands

To realize that this is unqualifiedly true, it is only necessary to recall the well-known fact that personal contact renders experimental thought-transference comparatively easy. The Society for Psychical Research has demonstrated this fact over and over again. Moreover, the therapeutic value of this method can be appreciated only when it is known that it is vastly easier to convey a therapeutic impulse by means of personal contact than it is to transfer a thought or a message; for the latter can be made available only after it has been elevated above the threshold of normal consciousness. It requires a good deal of psychic power to enable one to convey a telepathic message to another in such a way as to be understood, even with the aid of personal contact; whereas almost any one can, with that aid, convey an effective therapeutic impulse or histionic suggestion. The reason is that a telepathic message that conveys specific information to another must be translated, so to speak, into terms of objective experience; whereas a therapeutic impulse or histionic suggestion is expressed in the language of the soul, and it requires no translation to enable another soul to understand it. Hence it is that young children are susceptible to its influence to a very remarkable degree. Every sympathetic mother instinctively employs it to soothe the pains of her ailing infant, — ignorantly, it is true, but often with marvellous therapeutic potency. Every one recalls, with reverent gratitude, the soothing influence of the mother's sympathetic touch " when pain and anguish wring the brow." It follows that if this method of healing can be reduced to a science, so that it can be intelligently applied to old and young alike, by any one possessed of common intelligence, the best of nature's remedies will stand revealed.

It is my purpose in the ensuing chapters of this book to suggest a line of study and practice which, it is hoped, may result in discoveries that will invest so-called "magnetism" with its true scientific value. It may be recalled, by those familiar with my first work,[1] that I expressed a doubt of the correctness of the magnetic or fluidic theory, but expressed a preference for its methods when employed as a therapeutic agent. I was not then so well prepared with reasons for my belief as I am now, having since devoted nearly a decade, practically, to the study of the subject. The result is a practical confirmation of the views then outlined. The variations, if any are to be found, are in the details, and are the result of the correlation of the facts of physiology with those of psychology. I shall at least be able to show that the magnetic or fluidic theory is unnecessary; and it is an axiom of science that an unnecessary hypothesis is necessarily wrong.

If I succeed in this, another desirable result will have been accomplished; namely, the correlation of all the facts of mental therapeutics, showing that they all range themselves under the one supreme law of mental medicine, — Duality and Suggestion. Hitherto the adherents of the magnetic hypothesis have held that their system constituted an exception to the rule that suggestion is the prime factor in the production of therapeutic results. If this were true, it would show that neither hypothesis was correct, for nature's laws admit of no exceptions. One exception disproves a hypothesis with just as much scientific certainty as a thousand.

Again, if my hypothesis is correct, it must necessarily lead to a better understanding of the practical

[1] See "The Law of Psychic Phenomena," chaps. viii. and ix., "Hypnotism and Mesmerism."

methods of rendering the knowledge thus gained available for the uses of mankind. A knowledge of the structure of a machine is always necessary to enable an engineer to run it, and to keep it in repair and in continuous operation, with the least expenditure of time and energy. Without that knowledge one may succeed for a time in running a machine, but when it gets out of order he is at a loss to know the cause; and in his attempts to repair it he generally does more damage than good, to say nothing of his waste of time and misdirected energy.

The world is full of illustrative examples of this kind of engineering in the practice of mental therapeutics. Without the slightest knowledge of the fundamental principles of mental medicine, healers sometimes succeed in hitting the right spot in the machine to set it in motion, just as a small boy might accidentally open the throttle of a locomotive engine and set it in motion; the result in either case, good or bad, depending, not upon knowledge of the machine, but certainly upon " circumstances beyond their control."

To a certain extent magnetic healers are also handicapped. not by that crass and dismal ignorance which is the inseparable concomitant of superstition, but by their strenuous adherence to a hypothesis that is often misleading, and hence necessarily unsound. Nor is it because their methods of mechanical manipulation are entirely wrong, but because it is often misdirected, thus entailing upon themselves a vast amount of labor that is useless to the patient. Nevertheless, they are often successful in effecting cures that are little short of the miraculous; and this is presumptive evidence that their failures are due to misdirected applications of methods that are in themselves substantially correct.

It is my purpose to point out a system of practice by means of which greater certainty of results may be attained with less labor on the part of the healer. Based upon the undisputed psycho-physiological facts of science, the practice will be found to be simple to the last degree, and it may be successfully employed in the family by any one of ordinary intelligence; for nature has supplied the means for an inerrant diagnosis, and physiological science has long ago unwittingly revealed the exact locations where the stimuli are to be applied. I say " unwittingly," for the sciences of anatomy, physiology, and histology have been developed independently of medical theories or therapeutical hypotheses. Scientists have simply told us what the scalpel and the microscope reveal as to our physical structure, and left therapeutists to draw their own conclusions. It follows that no system of therapeutics can be complete when the great body of knowledge thus gained is ignored. I refer more particularly to those systems which depend upon material remedies, i. e., drugs and medicines; or upon digital manipulation or laying on of hands, otherwise, magnetic treatment, so called. Purely mental healing, or suggestive therapeutics, stands upon a somewhat different footing, for reasons that need not be here discussed. I desire to say, however, in this connection, that what is to follow in this book must not be construed as militating in the slightest degree against what has been said of the law of suggestion, or the potency of suggestion as a therapeutic agency. Suggestion plays its subtle rôle, for good or ill, in all systems of healing. It is a constant force or energy, which, like gravity, may be directed, but not evaded, — utilized, but not with impunity ignored.

There is, however, necessarily a vast difference in the therapeutic value of the different forms of suggestion, the effectiveness of each depending upon the mental condition which it induces in the patient. Hence it is that a form of suggestion that is effective in one case will utterly fail in another. It follows that the skill of the practitioner consists largely in his ability to adapt his suggestions to the exigencies of each particular case, — that is, to the mental status of each patient. Hence it is that in many cases under present practice hypnotism is resorted to in order to enable the operator to command the necessary mental conditions by shutting out all adverse objective influences or auto-suggestions.

I shall have no difficulty in showing that *histionic suggestion combines all that is valuable in all other forms of suggestion; and, moreover, that it renders hypnotism unnecessary in any case.* Not that the element of faith can be dispensed with in this process, but that it can be inspired with a certainty of results unattainable by any other process, and *in defiance of adverse auto-suggestions, or any other adverse influence whatsoever.*

The intelligent student of mental medicine will at once recognize this as the great desideratum in psycho-therapeutics; for all systems heretofore devised have been handicapped by the ever-present difficulty of securing the necessary mental conditions in the patient.

In a word, I shall attempt to show that the oldest, most effective, and, among primitive peoples, the most universally practised system of mental healing that history mentions, can be reduced to a science and practised intelligently: for it is founded upon a law of nature that is as universal and as beneficent as the love of God for his children.

CHAPTER II

THE PHYSICAL MECHANISM THROUGH WHICH MENTAL HEALING IS EFFECTED

Evidence for a Duplex Mechanism corresponding to Dual Mental Organism furnished by Anatomy and Histology. — Historical Sketch of the Science of Histology. — Cells and Cytods. — Unicellular and Pluricellular Organisms. — The Various Species of Body-Cells and their Functions. — The Body a Confederation of Groups of Cells. — Every Body-Cell a Mind Organism endowed with Intelligence Commensurate with its Function. — The Confederated Cells dominated by a Central Intelligence. — The Influence exercised by the Controlling Intelligence a Mental One.

THUS far in the history of the scientific investigation of mental therapeutics attention has been directed almost exclusively to the psychological aspects of the question. This was natural, for the simple reason that mental healing, as its name implies, is primarily a psychological phenomenon, and success in mental healing necessarily depends upon mental conditions. This being recognized, it was inevitable that the attention of scientists should first be directed to an inquiry as to the practical methods of inducing those conditions; and that was naturally thought to be a purely psychological problem. Besides, the light which the new psychology has shed upon that problem is so brilliant, and so satisfactory in its practical application to the subject-matter, that for the time being all other questions have been ignored as subsidiary, if not unimportant.

The fact remains that there are some very important questions relating to mental therapeutics that have not yet been adequately considered,—questions that reach the very heart of the subject-matter, both as to evidential importance and its practical value in the treatment of disease.

It is true that mental healing belongs primarily to the domain of psychology, and that without a clear understanding of the fundamental facts of man's psychological make-up mental medicine would still be and remain in the dismal realms of fable and superstition. But it is also true that the mental power which heals resides within the physical organism which is healed. It follows that if it is true that the bodily functions and conditions are thus controlled, there must exist some evidence of the fact in the bodily structure itself. That is to say, if the mind controls the body, it must do so by means of appropriate mechanism; and, in the absence of such mechanism, science would be compelled to reject all other evidence of mental control of bodily functions. On the other hand, if it can be shown that such mechanism exists, that it is co-extensive with the physical organism, and that it is obviously adapted to the uses of conveying intelligence from one part of the body to another, the evidence will be complete that the mind controls the bodily functions. Then, if it is found that there exists a duplex mechanism the functions, powers, and limitations of which correspond to what is known of those of the dual mental organism, it will constitute indubitable evidence of the scientific validity of our hypothesis of mental duality, and presumptive evidence of the soundness of the theory of mental medicine which we have outlined in Part I.

Fortunately, we have not far to look for abundant demonstrative proofs of the existence of mechanism especially adapted to the uses named. We have but to turn to any of the standard works on anatomy and histology, — sciences which investigate, respectively, the naked eye and the microscopic structure of the healthy body. And I desire to say, at the outset, that, in dealing with this branch of the subject before us, I shall not travel outside of the recognized paths of science as they have been outlined in the works of standard authorities. It is to histology, or microscopic anatomy, that we must look for the mechanism through which the mind controls the bodily functions in health and disease.

Histology, as it is now universally accepted, is a comparatively new science; that is to say, it is based upon facts of comparatively recent discovery. Like all other sciences, however, it is the product of evolutionary development. It may be said to have had its origin in the seventeenth century through the discovery by Hooke, Malpighi, and Grew. These scientists, making observations with the simple and imperfect microscopes of their day, saw in plants small compartment-like spaces, each surrounded by a distinct wall and filled with air or a liquid. To these the name *cell* was applied. During the latter part of the seventeenth and the eighteenth century these earlier observations were confirmed, and extended in various directions. No substantial advance was made, however, until Robert Brown (1831) discovered a small body in the cell which is now known as the *nucleus*. Five years later, Valentin observed in the nucleus a small body now known as the *nucleolus*. Schleidin, in 1838, adduced proofs to show that plants were wholly made up of cells, and attached special importance to the nuclei of cells. The next discovery was by Schwann, in 1839. It was he who originated the theory that the animal body was built up of cells, resembling those described for plants; and he defined a cell as a small vesicle, surrounded by a firm membrane inclosing a fluid in which floats a nucleus. This conception of the structure of the cell was destined, however, to undergo important modification. In 1846 Von Mohl recognized in the cell a semi-fluid, granular substance which he named *protoplasm;* other investigators observed animal cells that were devoid of a distinct cell membrane; and Max Schultze, in 1861, attacked vigorously the older conception of the structure of cells, proclaiming the identity of the protoplasm in all forms of life, both plant and animal, and defining the cell as " a nucleated mass of protoplasm endowed with the attributes of life." In this sense the term cell is now generally used.[1] The definition of a cell has been still further modified by the discovery that a nucleus is not essential, for none exists in the cryptogamia and in some of the lowest animal forms. In these exceptional cases the cell consists of a simple mass of protoplasm.[2]

Haeckel, however, does not recognize the lowest

[1] Bohm-Davidoff, Text-book of Histology.
[2] Green, Pathology and Morbid Anatomy.

forms of animals by the term cells; "for cells by no means represent the lowest grade of organic individuality, as that is usually understood." The cytods, for example, are "living, independent existences which consist merely of an atom of plasson, — in other words, of an entirely homogeneous atom of albuminous substance, which is not yet differentiated into nucleus and protoplasm, but exercises the properties of both united. For example, the remarkable monera are cytods of this kind. Strictly speaking, we should say, the elementary organism, or the individual of the first order, occurs in two different grades. The first and lowest is the cytod, which consists of an atom of simple plasson. The second and higher grade is the cell, which has been differentiated into nucleus and protoplasm." [1]

This, however, is a question of terminology which, for present purposes, is unimportant. The fact remains, as Haeckel proceeds to say, that " both grades, cytods and cells, are grouped together under the idea of sculptors or builders, because they alone in reality build the organism." That is to say, every living physical organism in this world is built up of cytods and cells; and this is the first salient fact which I desire the reader to bear in mind.

Before proceeding to discuss this matter in detail, however, I desire to remind the reader that all living animal organisms are divisible, broadly, into two classes, — namely, unicellular organisms and pluricellular organisms. The former. as the term indicates, are one-celled creatures, and represent the lowest forms of animal life, — the beginning of ani-

[1] Haeckel, The Evolution of Man, vol. i. p 130.

mal life on this planet, the earliest of man's earthly ancestors, the primordial germs from which all living creatures on this planet have been developed through the processes of organic evolution. The latter are simply aggregations or associations of the former; that is to say, pluricellular organisms are merely confederated associations of unicellular creatures, — a later development from unicellular life.

The unicellular organism was, and still is, the true terrestrial type of life; for it displays all the functions, in miniature, exhibited by pluricellular creatures, namely, feeling, motion, nutrition, and reproduction, the sum of which constitutes the idea of life. "All these properties which the multicellular, highly developed animal possesses, appear in each cell, at least in its youth. There is no longer any doubt about this fact, and we may therefore regard it as the basis of our physiological idea of the elementary organism" (Haeckel). In other words, there is but one type of life on the surface of our planet, and that is the unicellular; and this type is preserved in all the forms of life. The unicellular organisms are termed "protozoans." Pluricellular organisms are termed "metazoans."

It would be highly interesting to follow the phylogenetic development of the cell from the moneron to man; but that is outside the purpose of this book. It must suffice to say that the metazoans were at first simple aggregations of the protozoans; and the fact of aggregation does not seem to have modified the separate unicellular lives, for each retains its complete autonomy, performing all the functions of a separate life. Change of conditions, or mutations of environment, however, led to more permanent grouping, and compelled modification and differentiation of functions, until at length it became impossible to dissolve the bond by which the unicellular lives were united. Thus the way was opened for further differentiation of functions, and thenceforward organic evolution proceeded on those lines. That is to say, the moment that an aggregation of cells became a confederation, with its differentiation of cell functions and consequent division of labor, every further step in advance consisted in increased differentiation of cell functions and still further division of labor. As a result of a long process of such differentiation, the organisms of the larger animals and of man came to be composed, as we find them, of thirty or more different species of cells.[1] For example, we have the muscle cells, whose vital energies are devoted to the office of contraction, or vigorous shortening of length; connective tissue cells, whose office is mainly to produce and conserve a tough fibre for binding together and covering in the organism; bone cells. whose life work it is to select and collocate salts of lime for the organic framework, levers, and joints; hair, nail, horn, and feather cells, which work in silicates for the protection, defence, and ornamentation of the organism; gland cells, whose *motif* in living has come to be the abstraction from the blood of substances which are recombined to produce juices needed to aid the various processes or steps of digestion: blood cells. which have assumed the laborious function of general carriers, scavengers, and repairers of the organ-

---

[1] Stephens, Pluricellular Man.

ism; eye, ear, nasal, and palate cells, which have become the special artificers of complicated apparatus for transmitting light, sound, odors, and flavors to the highly sentient brain cells; pulmonary cells, which elaborate a tissue for the introduction of oxygen and the elimination of carbon dioxide and other waste products; hepatic (liver) cells, which have, in response to the needs of the organism, descended to the menial office of living on the waste products and converting them into chemical reagents to facilitate digestion, — these and numerous other species of cells; and lastly, most important and of greatest interest, brain and nerve cells.[1]   These cells are of the greatest interest and importance, for the obvious reason that they are the most highly differentiated of all the cells of the body, and constitute, respectively, the organ of objective intelligence and the means of communicating information from one part of the body to another.

Without going further into details for the present, it must suffice to say that each organ of the body is composed of a group of cells which are differentiated with special reference to the functions to be performed by that organ. In other words, every function of life is performed by groups of co-operating cells, so that the body as a whole is simply a confederation of the various groups. And, to the end that the body may act as a unit, these groups are connected, each to all the others, by lines of intercommunication, which, in turn, are composed of other highly differentiated and specialized cells, namely, brain and nerve cells. Not only are the

[1] Op. cit.

various groups thus connected by lines of intercommunication, but these lines reach, directly or indirectly, every individual cell in the whole organism. This is elementary; for everybody knows that when any part of the organism is assailed, information of the fact is instantly conveyed through the nerves to the "central office," so to speak, and there measures for protecting the part are as instantaneously devised and the appropriate commands issued. Thus. if one of the extremities is pricked with a needle's point, the cell thus assailed instantaneously conveys information of the assault through the nerves to the brain, which, in turn, issues its edict, through the appropriate nerve cells, to all the muscle and other cells surrounding the injured cell, commanding them to unite their forces and remove the part assailed from the point of danger. This sounds like an elaborate process, requiring considerable time to effect it; but it is just what actually happens when one's great toe is pricked and he jerks it away. It is called "reaction," and in a sense it is; but the remedy applied is the result of a series of mental processes, beginning with the message sent to the brain by the injured cell, and ending by the application of the united forces of the muscle cells to the removal of the injured cell from the point of danger. The time required is inappreciable to the unaided senses; but it does, nevertheless, require a measurable interval of time to initiate and complete the process, as scientists have amply demonstrated by means of instruments of precision. It is. therefore, a process, involving in its every step the exercise of intelligence and the employment of mechanism.

It follows, *a priori*, that every cell in the body is endowed with intelligence; and this is precisely what all biological science tells us is true. Beginning with the lowest form of animal life, the humblest cytod, every living cell is endowed with a wonderful intelligence. There is, in fact, no line to be drawn between life and mind: that is to say, every living organism is a mind organism, from the monera, crawling upon the bed of the ocean, to the most highly differentiated cell in the cerebral cortex of man. Volumes have been written to demonstrate that "psychological phenomena begin among the very lowest class of beings; they are met with in every form of life, from the simplest cellule to the most complicated organism. It is they that are the essential phenomena of life, inherent in all protoplasm." [1] It is, in fact, an axiom of science that the lowest unicellular organism is endowed with the potentialities of manhood.

I have remarked that each living cell is endowed with a wonderful intelligence. This is emphatically true, whether it is a unicellular organism or a constituent element of a multicellular organism. Its wonderful character consists, not so much in the amount of intelligence possessed by each individual cell, as it does in the quality of that intelligence. That is to say, each cell is endowed with an instinctive, or intuitive, knowledge of all that is essential to the preservation of its own life, the conservation of its energies, and the perpetuation of its species. In other words, it is endowed with an intuitive knowledge of the laws of its own being, which knowl-

[1] Binet, The Psychic Life of Micro-organisms.

edge is proportioned to its stage of development and adapted to its environment. Thus, the unicellular organism is endowed, antecedently to and independently of reason, experience, or instruction, with a knowledge of the ways and means of obtaining nourishment. A mass of unorganized protoplasm, it projects portions of itself (pseudopodia), and thus performs the act of locomotion in search of food. When food is found, it is enveloped in the mass of protoplasm, digested, and assimilated. It has the power of choice, for it rejects that which is unwholesome, retaining only that which is nourishing. It has memory, as is shown by the fact that, having once encountered danger, it will afterwards avoid it when presented under similar circumstances (Mœbius), or, having found food in one locality, it will afterwards seek it in the same direction (Gates). In fact, memory is one of the most elementary of psychological facts (Binet). It is susceptible to the emotions of surprise and fear, as is clearly shown by Binet's experiments with Infusoria. It has feeling, for it reacts to peripheral stimuli (Haeckel). It adapts means to ends, near and remote, as is shown by Verworn's [1] experiments with the Difflugia. And, finally, it reproduces itself by fission or segmentation.

Binet, in his preface to the American edition of his great work on " The Psychic Life of Micro-organisms," concludes a summary of the psychological properties of the lower orders of unicellular organisms in the words following: "We shall not regard it as strange, perhaps, to find so complete a psychology in the history of the lower organisms,

[1] Quoted by Binet.

when we call to mind that, agreeably to the ideas of evolution now accepted, a higher animal is nothing more than a colony of protozoans. Every one of the cells composing such an animal has retained its primitive properties, giving them a higher degree of perfection by division of labor and by selection. The epithelial cells that secrete the nails and the hair are organisms perfected with reference to the secretion of protective parts. Similarly, the cells of the brain are organisms that have been perfected with reference to psychical attributes."

The salient point to be observed here is that, so far as the physical sciences reveal the structure of man, he is composed wholly of confederated cells, each one of which has been developed and perfected with special reference to its place in the organism and the function assigned to it. Nor must it be forgotten that each individual cell is a mind organism, and that it is endowed with an intelligence commensurate with the duties it has to perform. Now, the one specific duty which each cell has to perform, under normal conditions, is to do its part toward the preservation of the life, health, and well-being of the confederated organism. Under normal conditions, that is, when no disturbing influences are at work, this task is performed easily and without friction; that is to say, in the absence of disease or traumatic disturbances, each cell is in perfect health and automatically performs its specific function without disturbing its neighbors.

But it has other duties to perform in which its intelligence is more pronouncedly in evidence. In case of disease or accident it is charged with the duty of repairing the organism and restoring normal conditions; and this it does with an intelligence and energy that savors of creative power. No one needs to be told with what promptitude and energy and intelligence nature sets to work to heal a wound or unite a fractured bone, under favoring conditions, mental and physical. No surgeon pretends to be able to do more than establish those conditions, and let nature do the rest; and every intelligent surgeon or physician will tell us that nature does its work of healing through the co-operative efforts of millions of intelligent entities, known to science as cells.

Nor will any intelligent physician or surgeon or biologist gainsay the proposition that these mind organisms are governed, controlled, and directed in their work by a central intelligence resident within the organism. Scientists may differ as to the proper terminology by which the central intelligence should be designated; but no one denies its existence, or its power to control its millions of subordinates. Thus, it has been called the " subconscious mind," the " unconscious mind," the " secondary self," the " subliminal consciousness," the " communal soul," the " secondary personality," etc., the various terms employed being governed largely by the point of view from which the subject is treated. I have designated it as the " subjective mind," for reasons which have already been set forth. Philosophers may differ in opinion as to its origin and its ultimate destiny; and biologists may not be agreed as to just what it is, — that is to say, whether it is the sum of all the intelligences of which the body is composed, or whether it is an independent entity capable of surviving the dissolution of the confederacy which it controls.

None of these questions, however, are at issue in this discussion; for the one salient fact upon which all who are acquainted with the propædeutics of experimental psychology are agreed, is that it exists, that it is an intelligence, and that it controls the functions of the confederated cells of the physical organisms of all sentient creatures. Even Haeckel, the great materialist, who apparently knows nothing of the new psychology, in discussing the third stage of phyletic psychogenesis, has this to say of what he calls the " tissue soul ": " This ' tissue soul ' is the higher psychological function which gives physiological individuality to the compound multicellular organism as a true ' cell commonwealth.' It controls all the separate ' cell souls ' of the social cells — the mutually dependent ' citizens ' which constitute the community."[1] This he holds to be true alike of plants and animals.

It is, however, a work of supererogation to dwell upon the obvious fact that a confederation of intelligences, organized for a specific purpose, must act in subordination to some central power or authority. Such a power is as much a biological necessity as an executive officer is a political necessity to a state or nation. In point of fact, the cell commonwealth is more nearly analogous to an irresponsible despotism than to any other form of human government; for the central power not only controls the organism as a unit, but it controls each group of cells (organ) and each individual cell in the whole organism. This

---

[1] Riddle of the Universe, p. 157.

is also a biological necessity, for there can be no legislative authority to share the power or the responsibility. That it is true is evidenced by the fact that the central power is in possession of the means of reaching not only each group of cells, but each individual cell in the whole organism. This subject, however, will be discussed when we come to point out the mechanism by which this is rendered possible.

In the meantime I submit that I have already shown that the physical organism is especially adapted to the reception of mental influences; for each particular part of it is a mind organism, every function of which is controlled by an organized intelligence. The influence exercised by the controlling intelligence is, therefore, a mental influence, pure and simple; for, in the nature of things, it can be no other.

13

CHAPTER III

THE PHYSICAL MECHANISM THROUGH WHICH MENTAL HEALING IS EFFECTED (*Continued*)

The Cerebro-Spinal and the Sympathetic Nervous Systems. — The Former controls the Voluntary Movements and is dominated by the Objective Mind. — The Latter controls the Involuntary Movements and is dominated by the Subjective Mind. — The Subjective Mind can usurp the Functions of the Cerebro-Spinal System. — The Objective Mind powerless to control directly a purely Involuntary Muscle. — A Nexus between the two Nervous Systems corresponding to that between the two Minds. — The Nerve Connections between the two Systems enable the Objective Mind to communicate its Therapeutic Suggestions to the Subjective. — The Pseudopodia of Unicellular Organisms. — Protoplasmic Filaments the Means of Communication between Body-Cells. — This is effected by Physical Contact. — The Nerve and Brain Cells highly specialized for this Purpose. — Being Mind Organisms, the Energy involved in the Transmission of Sensation is a Mental One.

NO one needs to be told that the nerves are the lines of communication through which the mind receives intelligence from, and issues its mandates to, every part of the body; but the special adaptation of the means to the ends is not so generally understood.

It is not my purpose to inflict upon the reader a lengthy dissertation on the subject of the nervous system of man, but to outline a few of the salient facts which bear upon the subject of mental medicine.

Before proceeding, however, to describe the structure of the nerves with reference to their functional activities as carriers of intelligence and therapeutic impulses. I desire to say one word in reference to the structure of the nervous system with reference to the theory of mental duality. Postulating a duplex mental organism, such as experimental psychology reveals, we have a logical right, *a priori*, to expect to find confirmatory evidence of the fact in a corresponding nervous organism. Accordingly we find that man is endowed with two nervous systems, — namely, the cerebro-spinal nervous system and the sympathetic nervous system. If, now, we find that the two nervous systems correspond in function to the known powers and limitations of the two minds, it will constitute conclusive proof of the correctness of the theory of mental duality.

Beginning, then, with the cerebro-spinal system, we know that, as its name indicates. it is presided over by the brain, the organ of the objective mind, and that it controls the voluntary movements of the body. On the other hand, the sympathetic system presides over all involuntary movements. such as nutrition, secretion, vaso-motor action, reproduction, etc. Its centre of functional activity is the solar plexis, sometimes called the " abdominal brain." [1] In using this term. says Dr. Robinson. " I mean to convey the idea that it is endowed with the high powers and phenomena of a great nervous centre; that it can organize, multiply, and diminish forces." [2]

[1] See Robinson on " The Abdominal Brain and Automatic Visceral Ganglia."
[2] Op. cit., p. 29.

I assume, of course, that the mental organism which presides over the sympathetic nervous system and organizes and controls its forces, is the subjective mind, although the dominion of that mental organism is by no means limited to the visible domain of that congeries of nerve ganglia known to empirical anatomy as the sympathetic nervous system. It necessarily presides over all the silent forces or involuntary activities of the whole physical organism; otherwise the latter could not act as a unit. Besides, the facts of psychology teach us that the subjective mind can under certain conditions, not yet very clearly defined, invade the domain and usurp the functions of the cerebro-spinal system. This may be brought about experimentally, as in hypnotism, or trance, induced or spontaneous; or it may occur in response to necessity, as when the body is in imminent and deadly peril.[1] In such an emergency the objective mind functions too slowly, and the nerve responses are correspondingly sluggish; and hence the subjective mind, ever alert for the protection of the body, instantaneously inhibits all brain mentation, seizes upon its mechanism of motion, and wields it with inconceivable rapidity and precision, often snatching the body from the very jaws of death. The difference in the action of the two minds in such cases is the difference between reason and instinct or intuition. The one requires time for deliberation, with its accompanying doubt and hesitancy; the other is instantaneous in mentation and appropriate action. Hypnotism, in this sense, is merely

[1] For a full discussion of this topic, see "The Law of Psychic Phenomena."

a method of inducing the subjective mind to inhibit the action of the brain, to the end that certain of its functions may be usurped by the subjective mind. When the inhibition is accomplished, " automatism," e. g., automatic writing, etc., is rendered possible, — which is but another way of saying that the mental organism which normally presides over the sympathetic nervous system, has assumed temporary control of the cerebro-spinal system.

This constitutes one of the points of radical difference between the powers and limitations of the two minds: the subjective mind may, and does on occasion, control every nerve and muscle in the physical organism, voluntary and involuntary; but the objective mind cannot directly control one purely involuntary muscle.

The far-reaching significance of this one fact cannot be dwelt upon here; but I cannot refrain from remarking, *en passant,* that it constitutes indubitable evidence that the subjective mind is the primary intelligence of organic life; the corollary of which is that the objective mind, with its organs, is the product of organic evolution. I make this remark for the reason that some scientists have labored to prove that the sympathetic nervous system is a subordinate offshoot of the cerebro-spinal system. I have incidentally pointed out this fallacy elsewhere [1] in discussing the facts of organic and mental evolution, the sum of which demonstrates that the subjective mind antedated the objective, or brain intelligence, by untold millions of years. That there is a nerve connection between the two nervous sys-

[1] See " The Divine Pedigree of Man."

tems is necessarily true; that they are intimately correlated is well known and admitted by those who most strongly assert the essential independence of the sympathetic. Experimental psychology teaches us that there exists a nexus between the two minds, enabling them, under certain conditions, to act in perfect synchronism. The same reason exists for an intimate interrelation between the two nervous systems. But as the subjective mind often asserts its independence of the objective, so are the essential functions of the sympathetic ganglia independent of control by the cerebral centre. They may be modified by indirection, as by suggestion, but the essential vital processes go on independently of objective will or desire. In other words, the life forces, which are presided over by the subjective mind, acting through the sympathetic nervous system, persist independently of the will or volition of the objective mind acting through the cerebro-spinal nervous system. As before remarked, it is only by indirection that the latter can modify the action of the sympathetic nervous organism: and this is where the law of suggestion presents itself as a therapeutic agent. The nerve connections between the two nervous systems enable the objective mind to communicate its therapeutic suggestions to the subjective mind. The latter, ever ready to adopt whatever measures promise to preserve health and prolong life, communicates the necessary therapeutic impulses, through the nerves, to the cell intelligences which are involved in the disease, stimulating them to increased activity, or the reverse, as occasion requires, — in a word, reestablishing normal metabolism in the diseased cells.

In this connection it must be remarked that the latest, most intelligent, and most comprehensive theory of disease is that *a disease of the body is a disease of the cells of the body*. The great German physician, Rudolf Virchow, recently deceased, has established this proposition beyond all peradventure.[1] Indeed it is, obviously and necessarily, the only theory of disease that is all-inclusive in its terms, and, in fact, self-evident. Its correlative is that the only effective therapeutic agents are those that reach the diseased cells and are capable of restoring them to normal activity. This is necessarily true whether the remedies are material or mental. It follows that the best remedies are those which reach the diseased locality by the most direct route and are invested with the necessary therapeutic potency, that is, the power to stimulate the diseased cells to normal activity.

I submit that I have shown one potent therapeutic agent, and exhibited the mechanism through which it operates; and I have shown the route over which its forces travel to reach the humblest cell in the physical organism. It is a mental power or energy; it transmits its mandates through lines composed of mind organisms; and the humblest beneficiaries of its prepotent energy are all mind organisms, — intelligent entities, capable of responding to every impulse from the central intelligence. I have also shown a bodily mechanism which renders the dual mind hypothesis a biological as well as a psychological necessity to any rational theory of causation. It remains to point out the specific structure of the

[1] Cellular Pathology.

nerves, considered as the instruments by which therapeutic impulses are transmitted and pain inhibited.

In doing so, it will first be necessary to refer again to unicellular organisms. In the amœboid forms of life — the ciliates, rhizopods, flagellates, and others — we find that the living cell, when leading an independent existence, has the power to throw out from its protoplasmic substance projections (pseudopodia) and filaments. The very lowest animal organisms, e. g., the monera, throw out pseudopodia as a means of locomotion, and in the more highly developed protozoans these projections assume a more or less permanent character, as cilia and flagella. It is by means of these projections that unicellular creatures take cognizance of their environment, seize their food, and communicate with each other. These filaments are themselves capable of feeling and moving in response to it, and are therefore composed of living matter.

Now, this power of projecting living filaments is one of the salient characteristics of the histological cells which constitute the vital units of all multicellular animal organisms. As in unicellular life, they are projected and retracted in pursuance of some want or emotion, and constitute the means of communication with neighboring cells. It is, in fact, the only means by which a sentient tissue results from their union. Moreover, it is by this means of intercommunication with each other that the millions of cells composing the body can exist as an individual animal, exhibit personality, and live, move, and have their being as one individual entity.

Now, as each cell in the confederation is differentiated with especial reference to its functions, it follows that the nerve cells are more highly specialized as carriers of intelligence than any others. Hence we find that the filaments are more distinctly in evidence in the nerve cells than in others, in that they have apparently assumed a more or less permanent character, — that is to say, under the now generally accepted theory that these filaments are the substratum of the nerve system. Be this as it may, it is certain that the nerve cells project these living tentacles from cell to cell, and that " in no tissue is this living connection so complete as in nerve tissue, and the gray cerebral tissue " (Stephens).

It is important, for more reasons than one, that we should here pause for a moment to consider this phenomenon in connection with the gray tissue of the cerebral cortex. No one needs to be told that the brain is the organ of the objective mind and the centre of the cerebro-spinal nervous system; or that the group of highly differentiated cells which constitutes the organ of intellect is located in the cortex, or outer surface layer or layers of the brain. The universally accepted theory is that the brain cells of the cerebral cortex constitute the storehouse of objective memory. Every cell, therefore, corresponds to some experience or thought of the individual; that is to say, for each new thought or experience of the individual, a new brain cell is developed or an old one modified. This theory is confirmed by the fact that the more highly men or the higher animals are cultivated intellectually, the more numerous are the convolutions of the brain and the deeper are the fissures, thus enlarging the cortical area and providing room for the constantly augmenting number of cells during the active or progressive life of the individual.

Now, each one of these cells is in either actual or potential communication with every other cell in the cortex, by means of filaments of living protoplasmic matter akin to those already described as pertaining to the humbler cells of the bodily organism. They differ in degree of differentiation, but not in function. That is to say, these filamentary projections from cell to cell constitute the means of communicating intelligence from cell to cell, whether they are the cells of the cerebral cortex, or the nerve cells of the body, or the humbler tissue or bone cells of the outlying frontiers of the physical organism.

I make these remarks here for two reasons: first, because materialistic scientists have racked their brains with an energy out of all proportion to results in an effort to solve the problem as to how sensation is communicated from cell to cell along these filamentary projections, whether by chemism, wave-motion, electro-motive energy, or by currents of particles of the cells themselves; and secondly, because I wish to make it clear to the reader that in dealing with man we are dealing with an intelligent entity whose whole physical organism is composed of intelligent entities — mind organisms — each one of which is endowed with intelligence proportioned to its place and function.

It is, therefore, superfluous to postulate any form of energy but mental energy, to account for the transmission of sensation from one cell to another. That is to say, it is obviously done by the transmission of intelligence from cell to cell by means of filaments projected from one cell until it comes in contact with its neighbor, — just as ants communicate messages to each other, and lay plans of co-operative action, by touching each other with their antennæ. Indeed, as we shall see in its proper place in this book, the communication of intelligence by means of physical contact is one of the most common of psychological phenomena. In the meantime I desire the reader to bear in mind the fact that the communication of intelligence by means of physical contact is the prime factor of sentient life; for, I repeat it. it is the one means of intercommunication between cell and cell that enables the vast congeries of sentient organisms to live, move, and have their being as *one.*

Besides, it must not be forgotten that all the cells of the human organism are descended from a single cell, the human egg-cell, which, " as soon as it is fertilized, multiplies by division and forms a community, or colony of many social cells. These differentiate themselves, and by their specialization, by various modifications of these cells, the various tissues which compose the various organs are developed. The developed many-celled organisms of man and of all higher animals resemble, therefore, a social, civil community, the numerous single individuals of which are, indeed, developed in various ways, but were originally only simple cells of one common structure." [1]

It will thus be seen that, according to one of the highest living authorities, not only is every cell in the body descended from a single parent cell, but that all were originally, that is, before differentiation

[1] Haeckel, The Evolution of Man, vol. i. p. 147.

began, "only simple cells of one common structure."
It follows that the essential characteristics and powers
remain the same in all, differing only in degree. Now,
the essential characteristic of the cell is that it is a
mind organism; and one of its essential powers is
that of communicating with its fellow cells by means
of the filaments we have described. The only question, therefore, is, Is the impulse thus communicated
from cell to cell a purely mental, intelligent impulse,
or is it some form of energy known to material
science as "wave-motion," "chemism," or "electro-
motive energy"? This question is easily settled by
showing that the cells of one group do communicate
intelligence to each other. If this can be shown, it
follows that all cells having a common origin, originally identical in structure, and possessing the same
structural facilities for communicating intelligence,
do the same thing in the same way.

It is scarcely necessary to say that the brain cells
furnish the necessary example. They have the same
origin, and were originally of "one common structure" with all the other cells of the organism. Differentiation did not change their essential nature as
mind organisms. It only modified their morphologi-
cal structure to adapt them to the performance of the
work assigned to them, and it endowed each with the
intelligence requisite to the performance of its special
work. In the distribution of assignments the brain
cells were exalted to a position of regal supremacy
and endowed with psychic powers commensurate
with their station. But they are no more perfectly
adapted to the performance of their special functions
than are the others to theirs. Each is endowed with

special powers, suitable and entirely adequate to the performance of its special duties; all are endowed with the instinct of self-preservation; each, in its own sphere of activity, is endowed with an intuitive knowledge of how to adapt means to ends in the conservation of life and in the repair of traumatic injuries; and all are subject to the volition of that central intelligence which, with never-sleeping vigilance, guards and guides the whole.

CHAPTER IV

THE MECHANISM OF INHIBITION

Analgesia Induced by Hypnotism or by Suggestion. — If Sensation is transmitted by Means of Physical Contact of the Filaments of the Nerve Cells, it follows that Interruption of Contact will inhibit Sensation. — These Filaments are retractile. — The Subjective Mind, by causing their Retraction, can inhibit Sensation. — The Phenomenon of Analgesia in the Presence of Death or Deadly Peril. — Catalepsy. — The Theory of Mental Medicine comprehended in the Words "Stimulation" and "Inhibition." — The Effects of Material Medicines mainly limited to these Two. — The Principle of Homœopathy. — Necessity for the Correlation of Psychology and Histology in the Study of Therapeutics.

ONE of the most wonderful of the phenomena with which experimental psychology has to deal is that of the inhibition of physical sensation or of pain. Everybody has witnessed it in others or experienced it himself, for it is also a very common phenomenon. It can be produced experimentally, as when suggestion is employed as an analgesic in surgery.[1] It happens spontaneously when one's limb is temporarily benumbed by a severe injury. It is in evidence when a raging toothache suddenly ceases in presence of the dentist armed with his instruments of torture. It never fails to manifest itself when one is threatened with sudden death by violence, as in the heat of a deadly conflict. The soldier rarely knows

[1] See Appendix I.

he is wounded so long as he is able to continue fighting. Often the first notification he has that he is
wounded is when he falls, weakened by the loss of
blood; and if his wound is fatal, he dies a painless
death.

Few have failed to experience the phenomenon in
some form; the most common being cases of temporary numbness resulting from wounds, and the
local anæsthesia or analgesia which almost invariably immediately precedes a surgical operation,—the
phenomenon of the subsident toothache being typical.
By far the most numerous class of cases, however,
occur in the practice of mental healing, especially
where the treatment involves the personal contact
of the healer with the patient; for example, in mesmeric methods, or the laying on of hands, or in some
forms of hypnotic practice. It is possible, however,
to inhibit pain by pure suggestion without personal
contact, as has been demonstrated again and again
under all so-called "systems" of practice in mental
therapeutics. The correlation of all the facts of all
methods has thus far given us the psychological formula which we have examined in Part I. of this book;
that is to say, it has taught us that the subjective
mind is endowed with the power, when it is incited
thereto by suggestion, to inhibit pain. This is undoubtedly correct as far as it goes. But it does not
go far enough to satisfy the demands of the present
inquiry, — which is as to the histological mechanism
involved in the inhibition of pain. and incidentally
as to some cognate questions collateral to the main
subject of inquiry.

The intelligent student will have already anticipated me when I say that we must look to the nerve mechanism through which sensations are transmitted from cell to cell, to find the means by which the same sensations are inhibited. Thus, we have found that sensations and intelligence are transmitted from one cell to its neighbor through filaments of living protoplasmic matter projected from one cell into physical contact with the other; that, in a nerve, this filamentary connection is made from cell to cell throughout its whole length. It is, therefore, solely by means of physical contact of one nerve cell with another that sensations are communicated through the nerves.

It follows that if one of the cells in a line of communication should withdraw its tentacles from contact with its neighbors, the line would be broken, and sensation would be inhibited with just as much certainty as if the nerve had been severed by the scalpel. That these filaments can be retracted is well known to every histologist. for they are a part of the living protoplasm of the cell itself.

That each cell of the whole organism is under the control of the central intelligence which presides over the vital processes, is necessarily true. Psychology teaches us that this central intelligence, which we designate as the subjective mind, " has control of the functions, sensations, and conditions of the body." Necessarily, therefore, it has control over each individual cell that constitutes a factor in the functional activities of the body; and since the nerves constitute the means of communicating intelligence and sensation to all the outlying cells of the organism, it follows that the nerve cells are under the more immediate control of the subjective mind than are the outlying cells. Manifestly, therefore, the subjective mind may, by an act of volition, cause every cell concerned in the transmission of sensation to retract its tentacles or filaments and thus temporarily isolate itself from all intercourse with its fellows. Obviously, therefore, this is the method and this the mechanism employed in the inhibition of pain.

Under this hypothesis much that is mysterious in the phenomena of inhibition may easily be accounted for. Thus, the general anæsthesia, or, rather, analgesia, incident to imminent and deadly peril, must be due to a general retraction by the cells of the filaments employed in the transmission of sensation. Indeed, this phenomenon and that of death may be correlated. The fact that death is always painless may be due to the same cause, the psychological crises in the two cases being identical. It is the inevitability of death, real or apparent, that induces the phenomenon; and it seems to be the universal experience of those whose doom is sealed. Thus, the criminal condemned to death experiences it the moment when all hope of pardon or reprieve has been abandoned. "His faculties are benumbed," testify his attendants, he becomes "calm and indifferent," and when the supreme moment arrives, he marches to the scaffold without a tremor to indicate that he is possessed of a nervous organism.

Closely allied to this is the local anæsthesia induced by the near approach to an inevitable surgical operation. This subject has already been alluded to, and need not be dwelt upon further than to remark that the imminence and inevitability of a great crisis seem to be the prime factors in the induction of the phenomenon. Its potential value as an analgesic in surgery is set forth at some length in Appendix I.

There are some reasons for believing that the cells themselves, under great stress of emotional excitement, have the power of initiative in the matter of inhibiting local pain. Thus, in cases of casual wounds, the parts are benumbed for the time being; and if the wound is immediately dressed, no pain is experienced in the adjacent parts. Later, however, the pain is experienced in full measure. This would seem to indicate that the cells adjacent to the injured parts, under stress of some emotional excitement, — let us say, fear or fright,[1] — withdraw their tentacles and " retire within themselves," much as some insects do when death threatens. After the stress of emotion has had time to subside, they resume their normal activities, and pain ensues. But they find that thousands of their fellows have been slain; and this entails unwonted duties upon the survivors in the way of eliminating the dead protoplasm and generating new cells to take its place. In other words, the process of healing must be carried on by the surviving cells, facilitated, perhaps, by antiseptic

[1] In reference to the possibility of inducing the emotion of fear or fright in micro-organisms, M. Binet, in his preface to the American edition of his great work on " The Psychic Life of Micro-organisms," has this to say : " M. Romanes, in his zoölogical scale, assigns the first manifestations of surprise and fear to the larvæ of insects and to the Annelids. We may reply upon this point, that there is not a single ciliate Infusory that cannot be frightened, and that does not manifest its fear by a rapid flight through the liquid of the preparation. If a drop of acetic acid be introduced beneath the glass-slide, in a preparation containing quantities of Infusoria, the latter will at once be seen to flee in all directions like a flock of frightened sheep."

conditions provided by the attending surgeon; and this increased activity necessarily increases the sensibility of the parts involved.

Catalepsy is another form of inhibitory phenomena which cannot be ignored in this connection. It was formerly thought to be a disease; but the better opinion now seems to be that it is a supreme effort of nature to give the nerves a much needed rest. This view is fortified by the fact that it accompanies severe nervous diseases, such as hysteria; and by the further fact that, if let alone and not harassed by the administration of restoratives, the patient rapidly recuperates during its continuance, and is convalescent when normal conditions are restored. It can be artificially induced by hypnotism, including the characteristic muscular rigidity; and the universal testimony of subjects who have been experimented upon is that the experience, short as it usually is in experimental cases, is equivalent to a refreshing sleep. It is, in fact, one of the most wonderful examples of the power of the subjective mind to inhibit functional activity; for the inhibition extends alike to brain, muscles, and nerves, and, in short, all the vital organs. In fact, there have been cases in which the suspension of the vital processes was so complete that it simulated death so closely as to answer all the ordinary tests; and doubtless many have been buried alive while enjoying the recuperative rest which nature provides, in emergent cases, for the overwrought nervous organism. One was made the subject of an autopsy, with most indecent haste, in the hope of wresting from his brain the secret of certain psychic powers that had made him famous in two hemi-

spheres.   An open letter was in his pocket, addressed
to the medical profession, stating that he was subject
to cataleptic seizures, simulating death.

It will thus be seen that the unprotected cataleptic
is in danger alike from ignorance and from science.
Ignorance is prone to bury him alive; and science
hastens to saw his head open in search of the secrets
of the soul.

This may seem like a digression, but the importance of the subject of catalepsy must plead my
excuse.   I have treated the subject more at length
elsewhere,[1] showing the danger involved, not in the
phenomenon itself, but in the fact that it has been
treated as a nervous disease, often fatal, instead of
regarding it in its true light, — that of a purely
psychological phenomenon.   I cannot repeat my observations here, without undue repetition, further
than to remark that the fatal cases are due either to
premature burial or an autopsy.   It is, in fact, a phenomenal manifestation of *vis conservatrix naturæ*,[2]
about which so much is said and so little intelligently
utilized in therapeutic practice.   It is, as before remarked, the result of a supreme effort of nature, in
cases of emergency, to give the whole organism a
period of rest and consequent recuperation.   In a
word, it is a striking example illustrating the wonderful inhibitory powers of the subjective mind.   In
the next chapter I shall attempt to correlate its facts
with the phenomena of natural sleep and others of a
cognate character.

In the meantime I have briefly, though I believe

---

[1] See "The Law of Psychic Phenomena."
[2] The preserving power of nature.

with sufficient particularity for present purposes, pointed out the physical mechanism and the process by means of which those inhibitory powers are exercised. And I may here remark that, in this and the preceding chapters. I have shown all the mechanism required for a complete working apparatus for mental healing; for the formula expressive of the work to be done in healing is as simple as that of the theory of disease. "A disease of the body is a disease of the cells of the body," says Virchow; and it rises to the dignity of a universal postulate when it is remembered that the body is composed entirely of cells. In like manner the theory of mental medicine may be comprehended in two words, namely, "stimulation" and "inhibition;" that is to say, all that it is conceivably possible for mental energy to accomplish, when operating therapeutically upon a congeries of mind organisms under its control, is to stimulate the sluggish cells to normal activity and inhibit the abnormal activity of the others. Manifestly this is all that can be done by mental energy; but just as obviously this is all that needs to be done, for it means the restoration of normal conditions to the diseased cells.

Can medicines do more? Clearly not. The real question, however, of interest and importance in this connection is, Can material remedies effect the same results independently of any aid from psychical forces? I think not.

Let me not be misunderstood on this point. I am not one of that numerous class of extremists who, having learned something of the potency of suggestion as a factor in therapeutics, are instant and in-

sistent in the declaration that the therapeutic value
of all remedies is due to suggestion, pure and simple.
Having learned, for instance, that the placebo [1] is
wonderfully effective in some cases, — many, perhaps, — the extremists jump to the conclusion that
all material remedies must be classed with the
placebo, the therapeutic efficacy of which is, of
course, due wholly to suggestion.

I am fully aware of the potency of suggestion as
a therapeutic agent. I am also aware that there are
many cases in which some form of larvated suggestion is necessary in order to inspire confidence or
overcome prejudice. Indeed, I know some physicians of high standing in the profession who never
administer anything in the form of medicine except
the placebo, accompanied by a vigorous suggestion
as to the expected results, firmly believing that the
therapeutic value of all medicines is due wholly to
suggestion.

Nevertheless, there are medicines that are efficacious in healing disease when suggestion as a factor
in the case seems to have been eliminated. I have in
mind two classes of cases which will serve as examples; there may be more, — I do not know.

The first is where the medicine contains the specific
pabulum, chemical or nutrient, adapted to the requirements of the cells involved. Cells may be starved
into inanition, and disease may result. It follows that
normal conditions may be restored by feeding them.
Indeed, starvation of the body is the starvation of
the cells of the body; and nourishment is the remedy,

---

[1] Any harmless substance given to pacify the patient, such as bread
pills, patent medicines, etc.

whether it is taken in the form of medicine under the directions of a physician or in the form of a " square meal " prescribed by the cook.

The other class of medicines to which I refer produce their results by indirection; that is to say, they have no therapeutic efficacy in themselves, but they serve their purpose by arousing in the cells the instinct of self-preservation, thus stimulating them to intense activity in an effort to eliminate the " medicine " from the system. This, of course, necessarily involves the use of poisonous drugs. Startling as this proposition may seem at first glance, it appears to be sustained by well-known facts. No one needs to be told that, when poison is taken into the system, " nature " makes a supreme effort to eliminate it, " throw it off " No histologist needs to be told that " nature," in such cases, is represented by the cells of the body. They do the work, sometimes successfully and sometimes not, — success, of course, depending upon the amount of work they have to do as proportioned to the energy they possess. If the amount of poison is great, the labor required to eliminate it is proportionately great, and they may perish before accomplishing their task; and even if successful, they may find themselves exhausted by their efforts and unable to perform their normal functions, at least for the time being. But if the amount of the poison is small, they may succeed in eliminating it, and still have a reserve force left sufficient for normal uses. The difference between the two cases is the difference between a fatal case of poisoning and one that is not. Obviously, in either case the cells were stimulated to unwonted activity by the presence of imminent danger to life; in other words, they were incited to activity by the instinct of self-preservation.

I should hesitate to apply these observations to any system of drug medication, did not the facts stand out so conspicuously that they cannot be ignored. Let us examine a few of them:

Hahnemann, the great founder of the homœopathic system of medicine. builded better than he knew when he announced the discovery of that "law" or principle of medicine which he embalmed in the terse Latin phrase, *Similia similibus curantur,* — vulgarly translated, "Like cures like." The real meaning is that any drug which, when administered in large doses to a person in health, will produce a given symptom, will cure the same symptom in a diseased person when administered in small doses. Nobody has ever been able quite satisfactorily to explain how it is possible that a small dose of any poison can have exactly the opposite effect of a large dose; but all opposition. in Hahnemann's case, was confounded, if not silenced, by the wonderful success which attended the application of the supposed law to actual practice. It is scarcely necessary to remark that this is not the only modern instance in which success in healing disease has been held to "demonstrate" the correctness of a theory of therapeutical causation; nor is it necessary to repeat my observations regarding the logical value of such a supposition.

The fact remains that Hahnemann was eminently successful in curing disease, and his following has assumed colossal proportions, in spite of the ridicule heaped upon the system on account of the infinitesimal doses prescribed. This is the vulnerable point against which its enemies have hurled their most effective weapons, whether of logic or of ridicule; and many of Hahnemann's professed followers now repudiate the higher attenuations which he prescribed. This, in my view of the matter, is an error on their part, in some cases at least, as will appear later. Others have repudiated his doctrine that medicine should be administered solely with reference to symptoms, holding that the seat and pathology of each case should be studied and medicine administered that will affect the organ diseased. In this they are undoubtedly correct. Others, again, repudiate Hahnemann's fundamental doctrine that his one so-called law of *Similia* covers all cases. Dr. Kidd, of London, holds that there are two laws governing the subject-matter, namely, *Similia similibus* and *Contraria contrariis*.[1]

Without stopping to examine these two alleged laws in detail, it must suffice to say that the declaration that it requires two laws to transform virulent poisons into beneficent therapeutic agencies is the logical equivalent of saying that neither of them is a law, and that we must look further for the true explication of the phenomena. Nature's laws do not contradict each other, nor are they uselessly multiplied, although it might well be supposed that it would require the concurrent potency of half-a-dozen of them to convert a deadly poison into a medicine in the common acceptation of the term, — that is, a substance possessing in itself a healing potency.

It is obvious that in casting about for a hypothesis

---

[1] See "Encyclopædia Britannica," art. "Homœopathy."

capable of explaining the therapeutic effect of poisonous substances, we cannot safely postulate direct and positive medicinal properties to deadly poisons, be the doses large or small. The chemical constituents of poisons are not changed by mechanical division. But I think we may safely assume, under the hypothesis suggested in the opening of this discussion, that the most virulent poisons may have an indirect therapeutic effect when administered in infinitesimal quantities.

Allow me to repeat. Poisons necessarily stimulate the cells with which they come in contact; that is to say, the cells are energized by the instinct of self-preservation, and they make a supreme effort to eliminate the poison from the organism. If the quantity is too great, the cells are either paralyzed or killed. If the amount of poison is small, the same instinctive energy is nevertheless aroused, and the same effort is made to get rid of the poison. If the amount is small enough, they succeed in eliminating it, and have a wide margin of reserve energy left for normal uses.

It follows that the smaller the amount of poison they have to contend with, the greater the amount of energy remaining in the cells. Hence the alleged superior efficacy of the high dilutions. If Hahnemann demonstrated anything in reference to his system, it was this, and he constantly insisted upon it as long as he lived; and the few that remain of his faithful followers all insist that the higher attenuations are the more efficacious. And it must necessarily be true if my hypothesis is correct. But if *Similia similibus* is postulated, the question will ever arise to plague its advocates, When, in the process of mechanical division, does poison cease to be poison, its chemical properties remaining constant? In other words, when, in the process of braying it in a mortar, does a poison which is destructive of organic tissue become a nutritive pabulum for the nourishment and regeneration of the living elements of organic tissues? The question answers itself, for everybody knows that the mechanical division of chemical substances does not change their nature. A teaspoonful of salt dissolved in a hogshead of pure water can be recovered again, as salt, without loss in weight or modification of properties.

It seems clear, therefore, that a valid working hypothesis explanatory of the therapeutic effect of poisons must take into account the fact that mechanical division does not change the nature of chemical compounds, and that a poison is still a poison, however minutely it may be divided. When these facts are taken into consideration, the conclusion necessarily follows that the therapeutic effects of poisons are secondary, that is, produced by indirection.

I submit that the theory I have suggested embraces all the elements of a valid and useful working hypothesis; for it accounts for all the phenomena relating to the therapeutical efficacy of virulent poisons, and it does not require the postulation of a manifest absurdity. Moreover, it is based upon the known facts of histology and experimental psychology. The former reveals the cellular structure of the body, and forces the conclusion that all diseases of the body are diseases of the cells of the body. The latter reveals the psychology of the micro-organisms of which the whole physical structure is composed, and takes into account that wonderful, sleepless intelligence which guards and directs the whole. It is safe to assume that if Hahnemann had been in possession of the facts revealed by these two sciences, the theory of *Similia similibus curantur* would not have been heard of through him; for it would have been then, as it is now, an unnecessary hypothesis. As it was, the facts seemed to sustain him, and he was justified in announcing his discovery and fighting his battles to the end. In other words, his practice was purely empirical, although he thought he had discovered a universal law of medicine. Nevertheless, it was a great step in the evolution of medical science; and he is entitled to the gratitude of mankind for that he has taught the medical profession the folly of administering medicines in heroic doses.

I have referred exclusively to homœopathy in this connection for the reason that that school furnishes the most numerous examples demonstrative of the fact that, for some reason and in some way, the most virulent poisons have a therapeutic value. Doubtless many, if not all, medicines, except those that furnish to the cells some form of nutriment, operate on the same principle. Take, for example, the old-school method of treating a torpid liver by mercurial remedies. Who can doubt that mercury is a poison which, for some unknown reason, naturally gravitates toward the liver; or that the hepatic cells make strenuous efforts to eliminate it, stimulated thereto by the instinct of self-preservation? That it is a poison to be gotten rid of, is tacitly admitted by the physician, who invariably orders a saline cathartic for that very purpose. Mercurial treatment of the liver is also illustrative of the change in practice, by physicians of the old school, in the matter of dosage. Thirty years ago, ten to twenty grains of blue-mass was not considered excessive in cases of torpidity of the liver. To-day the same physicians prescribe calomel in one-tenth grain doses, or even smaller; and experience teaches that the modern practice is the best. This also illustrates the main point of my contention; for the old-style doses of blue-mass would prostrate the average patient for at least twenty-four hours, whereas the modern dose, while it is equally effective, is not followed by the old-style aftermath. The reasons may be restated: The effort required to eliminate a large dose exhausts the cells, and time is required for recuperation before normal conditions are restored; whereas the small dose is equally effective in stimulating the cells to action, but the energy expended in removing the poison is so small that the cells have a reserve force left sufficient for normal uses.

I have introduced this subject, not for the purpose of exploiting a new and universal theory of medicine, for I disclaim an object so ambitious; but because I wish to make it clear to the reader (1) that there is a psychic factor in all healing agencies, mental or material: (2) that this factor is not confined to suggestion in the ordinary sense of the term: (3) that no system of healing, mental or material, can be hypothetically valid or complete that fails to take cognizance of all the psychic factors: and (4) that no system, mental or material, can be adequately comprehended without some knowledge of the histological structure of the physical organism.

The first three points have been sufficiently discussed for my present purpose, which is merely to suggest a method of investigation, rather than to exploit a scientific dogma. In reference to the fourth point, it is only necessary to say that, since Virchow's cellular theory of disease is now universally accepted, it follows that therapeutics, as well as pathology, must be studied histologically. And it would be like the proverbial play of " ' The Prince of Denmark ' with the part of Hamlet left out," to ignore the psychological powers, attributes, and functions of the cells themselves; for each one is, first of all, a mind organism, and it is differentiated psychologically as well as physically, with special reference to the place it occupies and the functions it performs in the grand confederation. It is an axiom of biological science that there can be no life without mind. In fact, there is no distinction between life and mind that is not, in the last analysis, merely verbal.

The cell is the unit of animal life. It is an intelligent entity. It is moved by mental impulses. It is actuated by mental stimuli, and undue action is inhibited by the same energy. The microscope reveals all this, and it exhibits the structural lines of communication between cell and cell and between the central, controlling intelligence and each particular cell. It follows that a system of therapeutics that ignores the psychology of the cell fails to take into consideration the prime factor of life and vitality, and is the equivalent of ignoring the existence of the cell itself.

Indeed, the psychology of the cell furnishes a common field of observation for all the schools of therapeutics, mental and material, and none can safely ignore the lessons that it teaches. If I were to assume the rôle of a prophet, I should predict that in that field will eventually be found the means of harmonizing all the schools; for it is obvious that it is only by the correlation of the facts of psychology with those of physiology and histology that the truth can be approximated. If any one of the sciences could be safely ignored, it certainly could not be psychology; for man is, first, last, and all the time, a psychological being, whose every fibre is made up of living entities, each one of which is endowed with psychological powers, performs psychological functions, and is controlled by psychological energy.

Is it not all but self-evident that it is because cellular psychology has been ignored by the medical profession, as a factor in pathology and therapeutics, that the healing art is one of pure empiricism?

CHAPTER V

INHIBITION AND SLEEP, NATURAL AND INDUCED

The Various Hypotheses advanced to account for the Phenomenon of Sleep. — The Power of Inhibition possessed by the Subjective Mind an Adequate Explication. — The Powers of Stimulation and Inhibition correlative. — The Alternation of Work and Rest a Law which pertains to all the Cells of the Body. — The Isolation of the Brain Cells from Contact with Each Other the Cause of Unconsciousness. — A Universal Law of Inhibition comprehended in the Formula "Segregation of Cells." — Natural and Induced Sleep identical — Hypnotism but a Concomitant of the Power to induce Natural Sleep.

I NOW resume the discussion of the phenomena of inhibition, for the purpose of considering the question, Does not this subjective power of inhibition afford a valid explanation of the mysterious phenomena of sleep, natural and induced?

Much has been written on the subject of cerebral anatomy and histology, and scientists are in practical accord as to the general structure of the brain and the functions it performs during waking hours. All are agreed that sleep is a condition of rest of the nervous system, during which there is a renewal of the energy that has been expended during the hours of wakefulness, and that sleep is promoted by fatigue of the nervous system. But no two of them agree as to what changes take place in the organism that produce the state of unconsciousness. Numerous hypotheses have been advanced to account for the phenomenon, but none have thus far proved to be in accord with all the facts in the case. Thus, it has been held by some that sleep is caused by cerebral congestion; that is, that the blood vessels of the brain are charged during sleep with an unusual amount of blood. Others have no difficulty in proving that during sleep the brain is in a comparatively bloodless condition, and that the blood in the encephalic vessels is not only diminished in quantity, but moves with diminished rapidity (Durham). The conclusion was that increase of blood pressure tends to produce wakefulness, and decrease induces sleep. On the other hand, Mosso has shown that the amount of blood in the brain during sleep is constantly fluctuating from natural causes and environmental conditions, and that it may be experimentally increased and decreased, within wide limits, without awakening the sleeper. Preyer held that it was due to the accumulation in the nerve centres, as a result of fatigue, of sarcolactic acid; but later experiments have demonstrated the incorrectness of the hypothesis. Pflüger labored to prove that a deficiency in the supply of oxygen to the brain was the cause of sleep: to which Professor McKendrick replied that such a theory implies that cerebral activity depends upon cerebral respiration, and that sleep must therefore be a kind of "cerebral asphyxia."[1]

In fact many other theories are extant, some of

[1] See article by Professor McKendrick, in "Encyclopædia Britannica," on "Sleep."

which postulate pathological conditions of the brain and nervous system to account for the phenomenon of unconsciousness. But it is safe to say that no hypothesis has yet been advanced that is sufficiently comprehensive to account for all the facts; and hence the present attitude of science is that of suspended judgment, awaiting further investigation.

The question, then, recurs, Does not the inhibitory power inherent in the subjective mind furnish a valid explanation of the phenomenon under consideration? It seems to me that the question answers itself in view of what we have already seen of the inhibitory potency of that intelligent, sleepless energy which presides over all the vital functions of the whole organism.

It would be a work of supererogation to repeat what has already been said relating to the inhibitory powers of the subjective mind, and the visible mechanism through which it operates, beyond reminding the reader that —

The subjective mind presides over all involuntary muscles, functions, and processes of the whole organism. Hence its power necessarily extends to every cell in the body; and, to be effective, it must include the power to restrain abnormal activity as well as the power to stimulate and promote normal functioning. They are correlative powers, and the existence of one necessarily implies the existence of the other, just as much as the power of an engineer to open the throttle-valve of a locomotive implies the power to close it. Obviously, in either case, the exercise of one power in the absence of the other would end in disaster to the machine.

The fact is, if we can once succeed in divesting our minds of all ideas of possible abnormal conditions precedent to sleep, and our imaginations of the glamour of mystery, romance, and superstition with which poets and other dreamers have invested it, we shall have no difficulty in correlating its phenomena with others not so mysterious, or, rather, not so conspicuously in evidence in their manifestations. To that end we must begin by keeping separate, in our investigations, the psychological functions of the waking brain cells and their physiological functions when considered as a part of the physical structure. We shall then no longer be awed by the phenomenon of insensibility, nor wrought upon by the idea of a mind blotted out, nor harassed by the thought that sleep is the " twin-brother," or even the half-brother, of death. On the contrary. we shall find that the phenomenon called sleep is merely incidental to the operation of a universal psychological law which pertains alike to all the cells of the body. That law is that, under normal conditions, rest must always alternate with work in all vital processes and phenomena, otherwise speedy exhaustion and death necessarily follow. This is true of all the cells, as before remarked. Even the pulsating heart, apparently working without intermission, is in reality not doing so, as there are short intervals of relaxation between individual beats in which there is no expenditure of energy.[1] The same is true of the other nerve centres, the continuous functioning of which is essential to life, — for example, respiration and the distribution of blood. Aside from these, all the

---

[1] Op. cit.

other nerve centres and their component cells enjoy comparatively long intervals of rest. And this is true, presumably, without reference to their waking functions. I say presumably, because the logical presumption is that all the cells which enjoy alternate periods of rest and work are governed by the same law. Besides, it is an inexorable rule of scientific induction that we must never needlessly multiply causes. I submit that there is neither a logical, a psychological, nor a physiological necessity for two hypotheses to account for the same phenomenon, — one for brain cells and another for other cells. The object of inhibition is the same in all cases, namely, rest; and the mechanism is the same, the difference being one of degree. That is to say, the brain cells are the more abundantly provided with filamentary lines of intercommunication. But their functions are identical with those belonging to the humblest cell in the physical organism: that is, they are the instrumentalities for the transmission of intelligence and sensation from cell to cell, thus enabling the whole to act as one. It follows that the process of inhibition is the same.

We have already seen that the retraction of these filamentary lines of intercommunication results in the isolation of the cells and the consequent induction of anæsthesia. In other words, the functions of the cells are for the time being suspended: they no longer convey intelligence or sensation to their fellows, and they are therefore, to all intents and purposes, asleep, — unconscious. I submit that if this is true of any one group of cells in the organism, it is true of the brain cells.

To the long-mooted question, therefore, What are the specific changes in the organism that produce the state of unconsciousness? my tentative reply is, *It is the isolation of the brain cells from physical contact with each other.*

Let us examine this question a little further with special reference to the brain cells, their functions, and their filamentary connections.

We have already seen that the cells of the cerebral cortex are the depositories of memories, and that they are connected with each other by filaments similar in kind, and presumably in purpose, to those which connect the other cells of the body with their neighbors, or coadjutors in functional activity. Roughly speaking, we may say, by way of illustration, that each cell is the storehouse of a memory of an experience, or, let us say, of a fact, that may in due time be used in connection with other associated facts for purposes of induction. But before kindred facts or memories can be brought into actual association, a connection must be established between the various cells which contain them; and this is the office performed by the filamentary lines of communication already described. These filamentary lines may be termed the instruments of mental association; and they account for " the tendency of a sensation, perception, feeling, volition, or thought to recall to consciousness others which have previously existed in consciousness with it or with states similar to it." [1] In a word, the brain cells and their lines of communication with each other constitute the physical mechanism of induction, of correlation, or of association of ideas; the tendency in an active brain being for each cell to establish

[1] Century Dictionary.

immediate connection with new and kindred ideas
and to refunction on lines already established. In
other words, these lines of communication constitute
the mechanism which enables the brain cells to act
as a unit, precisely as the filamentary connections
between the cells of the body enable them to act in
harmony, and live, move, and have their being as one.

As we have already seen, when the connections
between the cells of the body are operative, intelligence and sensation are communicable; but when
from any cause they are withdrawn, all sensation is
inhibited, anæsthesia results, — local or general, as
the case may be, — and we say that the body is
insensible. The cells are at rest. In like manner,
when the connections between the brain cells are
intact, the process of mentation goes on; memory
combinations are made and crystallized into ideas,
and we say the brain is active, — the mind is conscious, — the man is awake. But when the cells are
exhausted, and a period of rest and recuperation is
required, the connections between the cells are withdrawn, and the brain, to all intents and purposes, is
resolved into its constituent elements. It is then
simply a mass of unicellular organisms for the time
being, — an aggregation and not an organization, —
and, as such, it is just as incapable of thinking, or of
an interchange of sensations, as would be an equal
bulk of protozoans dredged from the bottom of the
ocean. The cells are at rest; the brain is asleep, —
unconscious.

I submit that this hypothesis, crudely and imper-
fectly as it is stated, affords a complete explanation
of all the facts pertaining to the phenomena of sleep.
I have not space in this outline to dwell upon the

particulars of the various phases of the phenomena, but the intelligent reader will supply the deficiency. In the meantime I have but to remark that it seems to indicate the existence of a universal law of inhibition, — a law which enables the subjective mind to meet all emergencies as they arise, in sickness, in health, in deadly peril, and in death. That is to say, it enables it to inhibit pain in surgery or in sickness; it enables it in health to give all the cells of the body the necessary periods of rest and recuperation; it enables it to take entire possession of the body when imminent danger threatens; and finally, it enables it to afford complete immunity from suffering in the hour of final dissolution.

The most wonderful part of it all is the simplicity of the process and of the physical mechanism by which all these things are accomplished. It may all be comprehended in the simple formula. *Segregation of cells.* It is this, together with the wide range of its usefulness, that stamps it as a law and attests its universality.

It will now be obvious to the intelligent student of experimental psychology that this hypothesis affords an explanation of much that is mysterious in the phenomena of hypnotism. Students of my earlier works will remember that, following Bernheim and Liébault, I stated that " there is nothing to differentiate hypnotic sleep from natural sleep,"[1] and gave many reasons for entertaining that opinion. They need not be repeated here, for they all pertain to phenomena occurring subsequently to the induction of sleep. In the years that have elapsed since the expression of that view I have never seen any reason

[1] The Law of Psychic Phenomena, pp. 179 et seq.

to change it, although it has frequently been controverted by those possessing only a superficial knowledge of the subject. It is now apparent that Liébault, whom Professor Bernheim credits with being the first to proclaim the doctrine, builded better than he knew; for if my theory of sleep is correct, natural and induced sleep are identical. That is to say, the same subjective energy that induces sleep in one case induces it in the other, — by the same process, and by the aid of the same histological mechanism.

No one now pretends to deny the fact that the sleep of hypnotism is induced by the subjective mind, acting in obedience to the suggestions of the operator; and everybody knows that the state is brought about by inhibiting the activity of the brain cells. That the subjective mind is charged with the induction of natural sleep is evidenced by the fact that insomnia is often cured by suggestion. It possesses the power, therefore, and as it is charged with the responsibility for the well-being of the whole vital organism, no good reason can be seen for making an exception of that which is most imperatively necessary to the well-being of the organism, — the rest and recuperation of the brain cells.

It will now be seen that if this hypothesis is correct, or approximately correct, both natural and induced sleep are robbed of their mystery. Natural sleep is seen to be nature's method of securing the necessary intervals of bodily rest and recuperation; and the power to induce and regulate it necessarily inheres in that sleepless energy which controls, subject always to the law of suggestion, all the other physical functions and conditions.

And hypnotism, or the power to induce sleep, is

seen to be, not a thing apart, not anything exceptional, — not a mysterious power, resident somewhere, for some occult purpose, and capable only of inducing abnormal conditions of body and mind, — but *a concomitant of the power to induce natural sleep.* It is governed by the same laws and restricted by the same limitations, and the same physical mechanism is employed in the same way to induce it; that is to say, it is brought about by isolating the brain cells from physical contact with each other, just as in natural sleep. In either case the different stages of sleep are due to their more or less complete isolation; and the variant phenomena in different cases, and at different times in the same subject, are due to the variant degrees of isolation in different departments of the cerebral cortex. This is a subject, however, which cannot be entered upon at this time; for it is believed that the intelligent student of hypnotism will have no difficulty, under this hypothesis, in solving the various minor problems as they arise. In the meantime my sole object has been to point out an efficient cause for the phenomenon of induced sleep and to correlate it with other similar states and conditions, with the view of showing that hypnotism is but one of the numerous phenomenal manifestations of that inhibitory energy which constitutes the conservative power of the vital organism. In a word, hypnotism is a subsidiary phase of the phenomenal manifestations of that energy. It is merely incidental to it, and not " a law unto itself."

CHAPTER VI

ANIMAL MAGNETISM, HYPNOTISM, AND LAYING ON OF HANDS

The Immediate Cause of Natural, Hypnotic, and Mesmeric Sleep the Same. — The Process and Theory of Mesmerism. — Braid's Experiments. — The Process of Hypnotism. — The Confusion in Terms and Methods. — Liébault's Formulation of the Law of Suggestion. — Suggestion regarded as a Universal Solvent of the Mysteries of Hypnotism and Mesmerism. — The Effects of Hypnotism and Mesmerism due to Different Proximate Causes. — Physical Contact the Essential Feature which distinguishes Mesmeric from Hypnotic Practice. — The Psycho-Histological Theory. — Historical Sketch of "Healing by Touch." — The Effects of this Process not accounted for by Suggestion in the Ordinary Sense of that Term.

ALL that has been said in reference to the cause of sleep, whether natural or induced by the processes of hypnotism, applies with equal pertinency to that induced by the processes of mesmerism or so-called animal magnetism. The obvious reason is that the immediate or efficient cause of sleep is the same in all cases, whatever may have been the visible means of inducing the histological conditions that cause or constitute sleep.

The parallel between hypnotism proper and animal magnetism, so called, practically ends here. Owing, however, to a defective terminology that has grown out of conflicting theories of causation, the distinction between mesmerism and hypnotism has been lost sight of by many writers.

The practice growing out of this confusion of terms has also served to obliterate distinctions, so that many who call themselves hypnotists in reality employ mesmeric methods in whole or in part, and *vice versa.*

It will first be necessary, therefore, to give the reader a clear understanding of what I regard as the true line of distinction, to the end that I may not be misunderstood when I undertake to make a practical application of the facts we have learned in previous chapters to the subject before us.

"Mesmerism" and "animal magnetism" are terms that are frequently used interchangeably, because they represent the same theory of causation. Hypnotism represents another, and a radically different, theory of causation; but both stand for methods of inducing sleep for experimental or therapeutical purposes. The differences, of course, are in the theories and in the practice under them.

The mesmerists, or animal magnetists, induce sleep by processes varying in detail, but consisting essentially of coming into personal contact with the subject, and concentrating the mind upon the work in hand. Contact is made, sometimes by the operator pressing the balls of his thumbs against those of the patient; sometimes by making passes over him, with or without contact with his person; but generally by gently touching him at various points, particularly on the head and face; and often by merely laying one hand upon the forehead of the subject and the other at the base of his brain. For the relief of local pain the hand is pressed upon the part affected, or gentle contact-passes are made over the same. But whatever the details may be, in the process of manipulation, *the essentials are personal contact and concentration of mind.*

The theory of Mesmer and his followers is that a health-giving fluid emanates from the operator and impinges upon the patient at whatever point the contact is made. This hypothetical fluid is the " animal magnetism " of which we hear so much and know so little. It is supposed, however, to be charged, not only with health and vitality in a concrete form, but to invest its possessor with dominion over his fellows in love, war, politics, religion, and commerce. At least so say the current advertisements of those who have it for sale in the form of " lessons " at so much per lesson.

To do the early mesmerists entire justice, they did not claim for the hypothetical fluid the wide range of power and usefulness that is now claimed by the charlatans into whose hands it has fallen. But their ideas were sufficiently extravagant to make it the vulnerable point in mesmerism, at least it was the point which science, as represented by the medical profession of the day. attacked with hysterical insistence, not to say, insensate virulence. It was the weak point in the armor of mesmerism, because it could not be demonstrated, — that is to say, the fluid could not be segregated. bottled. and analyzed. The therapeutic efficacy of the practice, however, could be demonstrated; but that fact apparently served but to increase the virulence of the attacks upon the fluidic theory. This view of the matter. however, can only be sustained by the presupposition that the average physician is violently prejudiced against any theory or system of practice that threatens to heal the sick without the use of drugs. Be this as it may, the fact remains that the medical profession waged incessant warfare against mesmerism, ostensibly because the fluidic theory was held, *a priori,* to be unsound and unscientific.

In the meantime the mesmerists fell naturally into the common fallacy of supposing that their success in practice was demonstrative of the soundness of their theory. Thus believing, they found no difficulty in identifying themselves with that numerous and highly respectable class known as martyrs to the cause of Truth; and, consequently hysteria entered as a factor in the controversy on the side of the mesmerists as well as on that of their opponents.

And thus the controversy went on for many years. The mesmerists constantly gained ground, because they could heal the sick; and their opponents as constantly lost ground because they were powerless to disprove the facts of mesmerism or its theory of causation.

In the meantime Braid, a Manchester physician of high standing and repute, became convinced of the genuineness of the mesmeric sleep and of its therapeutic value, but remained unconvinced of the scientific validity of the mesmeric theory of causation. In other words, he did not deem it incumbent upon him to deny the facts because he deemed the theory untenable; but, like a true scientist, he proceeded to institute a series of experiments to prove the one and to disprove the other. In this he partially succeeded.

He confirmed the sleep together with its therapeutic potency; and he demonstrated the fact that the sleep could be induced without physical contact with the subject, by simply causing the latter to gaze steadily upon a bright object held slightly above the level of his eyes. This process of inducing sleep was designated by its discoverer as "hypnotism," from the Greek radix *hypnos*, signifying sleep. Properly speaking, therefore, the word should be restricted accordingly; for it was coined, not to rechristen mesmerism, but to distinguish the Braidian process from that of mesmerism or animal magnetism. This distinction, however, was soon lost sight of by the successors of Braid, who held that his discovery had solved the whole problem of induced sleep and disproved the fluidic theory. Braid himself did not make so broad a claim, although he was as anxious as were his professional brethren to demonstrate the invalidity of that theory. He simply claimed to have discovered one method by which sleep can be induced without personal contact, and, consequently, independently of the hypothetical magnetic fluid. He expressly declared that his method was not identical with that of mesmerism, but he considered " the condition of the nervous system induced by both modes to be analogous," — both of which propositions are self-evident. He admitted that the higher phenomena of mesmerism could not be produced by his processes, for example, thought-transference, etc.; whereas by the mesmeric methods the phenomenon of thought-reading — or telepathy, as it is now generally termed — was very easily produced.

It will thus be seen that there is a very clear line

of distinction between mesmerism and hypnotism, as
the latter was understood and practised by its discoverer. The one required personal contact, and the
other did not. By the methods of mesmerism the
higher phenomena could be produced with wonderful
ease and certainty; whereas hypnotism, as practised
by its founder, was powerless in that direction. In
the light of later developments, therefore, it is self-
evident that the essential difference was primarily
in the methods of inducing the sleep, and that, so
far as Braid himself is concerned, he deliberately
threw away all that was distinctively valuable and
vital in mesmerism, labelled the rest "hypnotism,"
and invited Science to feast on the dry bones. He
was not responsible, however, for the misinterpretation of his work that immediately followed, nor for
the confusion consequent upon the misinterpretation.
The vital point in which his work was misinterpreted
consisted in the assumption, by the enemies of mesmerism, that Braid had disproved the fluidic theory.
This led to a confusion in terminology, in that the
word "hypnotism" came to be employed as a generic
term, definitive of all methods of inducing sleep, so
that, instead of distinguishing Braidism from mesmerism, it obliterated all distinctions. This, in
turn, led to a deplorable mixing of methods. so
that hypnotists were prone to employ mesmeric
methods in conjunction with those of hypnotism
proper; and mesmerists often employed the hypnotic
process because of its greater facility in inducing
sleep.

The result was that mesmerists gradually lost the
power to produce the higher phenomena which dis-

tinguished their performances when the old methods were exclusively employed.

In the meantime Braidism gradually gained a standing among the medical profession of Continental Europe; and this eventually led to the formulation of the law of suggestion, as applied to hypnotism. That is to say, it was discovered that persons in the hypnotic state are constantly amenable to control by the subtle power of suggestion: and the law was thus formulated by Liébault, of Nancy. It has since been discovered, however, that the law not only applies to hypnotized persons, but that it is a general law[1] of the subjective mind, without restriction as to particular states or conditions of the objective mind.

Nevertheless, limited as it was supposed to be to the hypnotic state, it threw a flood of light upon the phenomena of both hypnotism and mesmerism. The result was that in a very short time there sprang up a school of hypnotism (Nancy) which taught that all that is mysterious about either hypnotism or mesmerism found a universal solvent in suggestion. This, of course, served to confuse the public mind still further as to methods, and to obliterate distinctions as to causation. Thus, the ultra-suggestionists held that all that was supposed to distinguish mesmerism from hypnotism was easily explicable by reference to suggestion; that physical contact was but a form of larvated suggestion; that passes served but the one purpose of inspiring confidence, having no therapeutic value beyond the suggestion embraced

[1] See "The Law of Psychic Phenomena," where it was first generalized as a universal law.

in the act: that digital manipulation of any kind owed its therapeutic efficiency solely to suggestion; and many went so far as to include all material remedies in the category of larvated suggestions.

I have already pointed out the fallacy of this belief so far as material remedies are concerned. Elsewhere [1] I have pointed out the fact that Braid's experiments demonstrated that adults could be hypnotized by his methods when suggestion in any form was out of the question; and the records of mesmerism are overflowing with evidence of the fact that many of its most important phenomena are produced under circumstances that exclude oral suggestion, or its equivalents, as a factor in the case. For instance, the fact that some animals can be mesmerized, and others hypnotized, demonstrates the absence, in both cases, of either oral suggestion, or any form of larvated suggestion that appeals to the intelligence of the subject. Moreover, the fact that young children can be successfully treated by mesmeric methods, and not by the processes of hypnotism proper, is demonstrative of the fact, not only that oral suggestion, or its equivalents, does not enter as a factor in either case, but that the effects of mesmerism and of hypnotism are due to radically and essentially different proximate causes. Again, what is of equal or of greater interest and importance, it demonstrates the vastly wider range of usefulness of mesmerism over hypnotism.

The questions, therefore, still remaining unanswered are —

[1] See "The Law of Psychic Phenomena," where this and cognate subjects are more fully treated.

1. What are the points of essential difference in the practice of hypnotism and mesmerism?

In answer to this, however, it may be safely assumed that, broadly speaking, physical contact is the one essential feature of mesmeric practice that distinguishes it from that of hypnotism. At least it is the only visible, tangible difference; and it is tacitly assumed to be the only difference by the enemies of mesmerism who have sought to show that physical contact is unnecessary.

2. The second question, then, is, What is the rationale of the therapeutic potency of physical contact?

This question reintroduces the old problem of fluidic emanations, or the theory of animal magnetism; for thus far but two hypotheses have been advanced to account for the phenomena. One is the theory of suggestion, and the other is the theory of fluidic emanations. I purpose introducing another hypothesis, based upon the correlated facts of psychology and histology, which may be provisionally termed the psycho-histological theory, or the theory of direct mental action upon the cells involved.

I have shown that suggestion, in the ordinary sense of the term, cannot be invoked to account for the phenomena incident to personal contact; and as this will more fully appear as we proceed, I shall provisionally dismiss it as untenable.

This leaves the fluidic theory alone to be discussed in connection with my own interpretation of the phenomena. This I shall undertake in the following chapter. In the meantime I desire to impress upon the mind of the reader that no theory invoked to explain the results of personal contact with the patient in the practice of mesmerism can possess the slightest claim to validity if it is not also applicable to the innumerable cases recorded in history, and handed down by tradition, of healing by touch, or the laying on of hands. For if there is a principle or law of nature underlying the phenomena as shown in mesmerism, it follows that all methods of healing in which physical contact is the essence of the process are governed by the same law.

In order to give the reader a faint idea of its antiquity, its potency as a therapeutic agency, the wide range of its usefulness to mankind in the past, and its potentialities when the principle underlying it is once understood, I condense Ennemoser's historical sketch of healing by touch or the laying on of hands: [1] —

The healing of the sick by touch and the laying on of hands, says that indefatigable historian of ancient methods of healing, is to be found among the earliest nations, — among the Indians, the Egyptians, and especially among the Jews. In Egypt, sculptures have been found where "one hand is represented on the stomach and the other on the back." [2] Even the Chinese, according to the accounts of the early missionaries (Athanasius Kircher, "China illustrata"), healed sickness by the laying on of hands. In the Old Testament we find numerous examples, of which a few are selected.

When Moses found his end approaching, he prayed

[1] See Howitt's translation of Ennemoser's "History of Magic," vol. i. pp. 109 et seq. (Bohn's Scientific Library).

[2] I desire the reader to make a mental note of this fact in view of what is to follow when we come to treat of the practical methods of healing by digital manipulation.

for a worthy successor, and we find the following passage (Numbers xxvii. 18, 20) : " And the Lord said unto Moses. Take thee Joshua the son of Nun, a man in whom is the spirit, and lay thine hand upon him. . . . And thou shalt put some of thine honor upon him, that all the congregation of the children of Israel may be obedient."

Another instance is to be found in the healing of the seemingly dead child by Elisha, who stretched himself three times upon the child, and called upon the Lord. The manner in which Elisha raised the dead son of the Shunamite woman is still more remarkable. He caused Gehazi to proceed before him to lay his staff upon the face of the dead child. This, however, proved to be of no avail. for reasons which will be stated in their proper place hereinafter. But when Elisha went up into the room, and laid himself upon the child, etc., and his hands upon the child's hands, so that the child's body became warm again, the child opened its eyes.

The New Testament is particularly rich in examples of the efficacy of laying on of hands. " Neglect not the gift that is in thee, which was given thee by prophecy, with the laying on of the hands of the presbytery" (1 Timothy iv. 14), is a principal maxim of the Apostles, for the practical use of their powers for the good of their brethren in Christ.

In St. Mark we find (xvi. 18), " They shall lay hands on the sick, and they shall recover." St. Paul was remarkable for his powers: "And it came to pass that the father of Publius lay sick of a fever and of a bloody flux; to whom Paul entered in, and prayed, and laid his hands on him, and healed him " (Acts xxviii. 8). "And Ananias went his way, and entered into the house; and putting his hands on him, said. Brother Saul, the Lord, even Jesus, that appeared unto thee in the way as thou camest hath sent me that thou mightest receive thy sight and be filled with the Holy Ghost. And immediately there fell from his eyes as it had been scales, and he received sight" (Acts ix. 17, 18). In St. Mark we find: "And they brought young children to him, that he should touch them; and his disciples rebuked those that brought them. But when Jesus saw it he was much displeased, and said unto them. Suffer the little children to come unto me, . . . for of such is the kingdom of God. . . . And he took them up in his arms, put his hands upon them, and blessed them" (Mark x. 13–16). "And they bring unto him one that was deaf, and had an impediment in his speech; and they beseech him to put his hand upon him. And he took him aside from the multitude, and put his fingers into his ears. and he spit. and touched his tongue; and, looking up to heaven, he sighed, and saith unto him, Ephphatha, that is, Be opened. And straightway his ears were opened, and the string of his tongue was loosed, and he spake plain" (Mark vii. 32, 35).

Numerous other passages are found in the New Testament all testifying to the wonderful therapeutic efficacy of laying on of hands. Some of them are clearly indicative of the superiority of that method over all other processes of mental healing. Thus, we are told that when Jesus visited his native village he did not do many mighty works there " because of their unbelief." But Mark, in relating the circumstance, adds this significant statement: "And he could there do no mighty work, *save that he laid his hands upon a few sick folk, and healed them*" (Mark vi. 5). The true significance of this remark seems never to have been appreciated. It means that the unbelief of the people prevented him from healing them (auto-suggestion) or performing any other wonderful work in their presence, except when he laid his hands upon them. Of this, however, we shall take occasion to speak more at length at the proper time.

Resuming the thread of Ennemoser's summary, we find that St. Patrick, the Irish apostle, healed the blind by laying his hands upon them. St. Bernard is said to have restored eleven blind persons to sight, and eighteen lame persons to the use of their limbs, in one day at Constance. At Cologne he healed twelve lame, caused three dumb persons to speak, and ten who were deaf to hear. The miracles of SS. Margaret, Katherine, Elizabeth, Hildegarde, and especially the miraculous cures of the two holy martyrs, Cosmas and Damianus, belong to this class. Among others, they freed the Emperor Justinian from a sickness that was supposed to be incurable. St. Odilia embraced a leper, who was shunned by all men, in her arms, warmed him, and restored him to health.

Remarkable above all others are those cases where persons who were at the point of death have recovered by holy baptism or extreme unction. The Emperor Constantine is one of the most singular examples. Pyrrhus, king of Epirus, had the power of assuaging colic and affections of the spleen by laying the patients on their backs and passing his great toe over them. The Emperor Vespasian cured nervous affections, lameness, and blindness, solely by the laying on of his hands (Suelin, Vita Vespas.). According to Cœlius Spartianus, Hadrian cured those afflicted with dropsy by touching them with the points of his fingers, and himself recovered from a violent fever by similar treatment. King Olaf healed Egill on the spot by merely laying his hands upon him and singing proverbs (Edda, p. 216). The kings of England and France cured diseases of the throat (goitre) by touch. It is said that the pious Edward the Confessor, and in France that Philip the First, were the first who possessed the power. The formula used on such occasions was, " Le roi te touche, allez et guerrisses," so that the word was connected with the act of touching, — physical contact. In England the disease was called the King's Evil: and in France the power was retained until within the memory of men now living.

Among the German princes this curative power was ascribed to the Counts of Hapsburg, and they were also able to cure stammering by a kiss. Pliny says, " There are men whose whole bodies are possessed of medicinal properties, as the Marsi, the Psyli, and others, who cure the bite of serpents merely by the touch." In later times the Salmadores and Ensalmadores of Spain became very celebrated, who healed almost all diseases by prayer, laying on of hands, and by the breath. In Ireland, Valentine Greatrakes cured at first king's evil by laying on of hands; later, fever, wounds, tumors, gout, and at length all diseases. In the seventeenth century the gardener Levret and the notorious Streeper performed cures in London by stroking with the hand. In a similar manner cures were performed by Michael Medina, and the child of Salamanca; also Marcellus Empiricus (Sprengel, Gesch. der Med., part ii. p. 179). Richter, an inn-keeper at Royen, in Silicia, cured, in the years 1817–18, many thousands of sick persons in the open fields, by touching them with his hands. Under the Popes, laying on of the hands was called Chirothesy. Diepenbroek wrote two treatises on it; and, according to Lampe, four-and-thirty Chirothetists were declared to be holy.

The foregoing comprise but a small part of the recorded instances illustrating the efficacy of healing by touch, or laying on of hands, as practised in all the ages. But enough has been said to show that the process is something apart from suggestion in the ordinary sense of the term. It is neither oral suggestion nor any of its equivalents. It is not larvated suggestion, for that implies an element of deception. Nor is it mental suggestion in the telepathic sense, — that is, thought-transference at a distance or without personal contact with the patient. All these forms of suggestion are now well known to those who practise suggestive therapeutics; and constant efforts have been made to correlate the facts of mesmerism with one or another of these forms of suggestion. But practical mesmerists well know that there are phenomena arising from personal contact with the patient that refuse to range themselves under either of the known forms of suggestion. Hence the strength and pertinacity with which they have held to the fluidic theory, the theory of animal magnetism. To do them entire justice it must be said that there is much to sustain the fluidic theory, especially in the absence of any means of disproving it, or of any more rational substitute. In the first place it was formulated long before the potency of mental action upon the bodily functions was more than faintly recognized. Secondly, the phenomena attending personal contact with the patient seemed to present some analogies to those of magnetic attraction and repulsion. Thirdly, those who opposed the magnetic theory offered no valid reason for so doing beyond the *a priori* assertion that it was " contrary to the nature of things," — a very dangerous weapon, by the way, for a logician to handle in the absence of proof that he is thoroughly acquainted with " the nature of things." Fourthly, when, at length, a substitute was offered in the newly discovered law of suggestion, it was found not to possess the essentials of a valid working hypothesis for mesmerism, for that it did not account for all the facts. They had, therefore, a logical right to reject it, provisionally at least, whatever may be said of their own logical attitude in seeking to account for the unknown by referring it to something still more unknown. Be that as it may, they have the right to demand a substitute for their own theory which will at least render the latter unnecessary.

It is my purpose in the ensuing chapters to offer such a substitute. Not, I hasten to say, one that will eliminate suggestion as a factor in any method of mental healing, — for that is obviously impossible if suggestion is a universal law of mental medicine, — but one that will reveal a form of suggestion, hitherto unrecognized, that is more direct and potent in its effects than any other form known to science.

CHAPTER VII

THOUGHT–TRANSFERENCE BY ANTS AND BEES BY MEANS OF PHYSICAL CONTACT

The Psycho-Histological Theory of Mental Therapeutics. — Communication of Mental Impulses by Means of Physical Contact an Elementary Fact of Psychology. — The Vital Units of Pluricellular Organisms habitually communicate by this Means. – Unicellular Organisms, grouped together in Colonies, communicate in the same Way. — Communication between Ants by Contact of Antennæ.— Hypothetical "Langage Antennal" of Huber. — Antennal Communion among Bees. — Inadequacy of Tactile-Signal Hypothesis. — Thought-Transference the Obvious Explanation.

BRIEFLY stated, my theory is that the effects ascribed to mesmeric methods, or, generically speaking, to the laying on of hands, are due to therapeutic impulses conveyed directly from the mind of the operator to the diseased cells in the patient, the connection being established by bringing into physical contact the peripheral nerve terminals of the two personalities. At first glance this may be, to many, a startling proposition but it is a question of fact, to be settled by evidence, and not a matter of philosophical speculation. Fortunately, the evidence required in this case is very simple and easy to find, but two questions of fact being involved.

The first is whether it is possible for one person to communicate intelligence, sensation, or therapeutic impulses to another by means of thought-transference, rapport being established by physical contact.

The second is whether the requisite mechanism exists to enable therapeutic impulses, thus conveyed, to reach the diseased cells wherever they may be located.

In regard to the first question, I have already shown that the ability of sentient creatures to communicate intelligence, sensations, or mental impulses by means of physical contact is one of the most elementary facts of psychology. I have shown that physical contact of cell with cell by means of protoplasmic threads or filaments is the one prepotent cause, or condition precedent to the manifestation of life and intelligence in all pluricellular organisms; that in the absence of these filamentary connections man would be nothing more than a congeries of cell tribes, — a huge amœboid mass, sentient, but not intelligent, — an aggregation, but not a confederation, of intelligent entities; and that mental unconsciousness as well as physical insensibility is the sure result of withdrawing these filamentary lines of communication between the cells.

This, of course, does not prove that one person can thus affect the cells of another by means of personal contact, but it is here mentioned (1) because the power to heal disease by physical contact must necessarily include the power to reach and control the diseased cells wherever they may be located; and (2) because the effectiveness of the mechanism employed, whether it be actuated from within or from without, is due wholly to the fact that the sentient beings which compose it possess the power to communicate intelligence, sensations, or impulses to each other by means of physical contact. Besides, this is one of the steps necessary to prove my assertion that the ability of sentient creatures to communicate intelligence to each other by means of physical contact is one of the most elementary facts in psychology.

In further proof of this I again refer to Binet's " The Psychic Life of Micro-organisms." In speaking of the fact that unicellular organisms are often found grouped into colonies, each temporarily acting as a unit, our author says : —

" In the genus Volvox colonies are found of which the structure is very complicated. Such are the great green balls formed by the aggregation of diminutive organisms, which form the surface of the sphere, and are joined together by their envelopes ; they have each two flagella, which pass through the enclosing membrane and swing unimpeded on the outside ; the envelopes, each tightly holding the other, form hexagonal figures exactly like the cells of a honeycomb. Each volvox is at liberty within its own envelope ; but it *projects protoplasmic extensions* which pass through its cuticle and *place it in communication with its neighbor.* It is probable that these protoplasmic filaments act like so many telegraphic threads to establish a *network of communication* among all the individuals of the same colony : *it is necessary,* in fact, that these diminutive organisms *be in communication with each other* in order that their flagella may move in unison and that *the entire colony may act as a unit and in obedience to a single impulse.*" (The italics are mine.)

The conclusion at which M. Binet arrives is that the ability of micro-organisms to communicate intelligence to each other by means of physical contact is

conclusive evidence " that their movements are reg-
ulated by the action of a diffused nervous system
present in the protoplasm."

This is a very just conclusion; for if it were not
true, the axiom of evolutionary science, that " the
potentialities of manhood reside in the lowest unicellular organism," would be but an empty phrase,
devoid of any biological significance. In other words,
there must be a diffused nervous system in the protoplasm of every unicellular organism from which
to develop a structural nervous organism in the
metazoan.

Reversing the order of statement of propositions,
the foregoing is the equivalent of saying, *a priori,*
that, " given a nervous organism, diffused or structural, in any sentient creature, it follows that, other
conditions being favorable, it can communicate intelligence to its fellows by means of physical contact.
If, now, this proposition is sustained by *a posteriori*
proofs, we may safely bank upon it as a fact in nature
which demonstrates our thesis.

Thus far, then, I have shown that the vital units
of pluricellular organisms habitually communicate
with each other, and that unicellular organisms, when
grouped together in colonies, communicate with each
other in the same way. It remains to show that some
pluricellular organisms can and do hold intelligent
communion with each other under identical conditions. namely. physical contact.

To this end we will begin by obeying the scriptural
injunction: " Go to the ant, consider her ways, and
be wise." In doing so I shall avail myself largely
of Romanes' so-called " complete *résumé* of all the

more important facts of animal intelligence" [1] known to science at the time he wrote. From this we learn, first, that the sense of sight in ants is extremely limited ; secondly, that they are destitute of the sense of hearing, and, thirdly, that they have some very complete and perfect means of communicating intelligence to each other. Their senses of taste and smell are very acute, and of course very useful to them for certain definite purposes But they are obviously not adapted to the communication of intelligence to the extent required to enable them to conduct the complicated system of social and political government which distinguishes them. Sight, hearing, taste, and smell being excluded from consideration, there remains but the one physical sense of feeling to which we can ascribe the power to communicate intelligence. The one observable fact that gives color to this supposition is that they bring themselves into physical contact with each other by means of their antennæ whenever an emergency arises requiring a consultation, or necessitating the issuance of a command. But the question at once arises, Is the sense of touch, *per se*, equal to an explanation of all the facts relating to the conveyance of the intelligence required to organize and administer a complicated system of governmental polity, to adjust social relations, to maintain discipline in war and enforce a division of labor in peace, to organize and maintain an army of offence and defence, to discipline its forces and command it in action, to build bridges and construct pontoons and ferries for the passage of vast armies over streams otherwise impassable, to invade successfully

[1] See " Animal Intelligence," Appletons' ed

the domains of foreign tribes and capture and enslave their inhabitants, and, finally, to inaugurate and maintain a system of slave labor vastly more successful, and, let us hope, more humane, than any that has ever prevailed in the history of mankind? All this, and much more, is to be accounted for on some hypothesis involving the transmission of intelligence between the units of this vast and complicated organization. I am willing, for the sake of the argument, to concede all that can reasonably be claimed for natural selection or survival of the fittest as a factor in the evolution of such a system. But there still remains the fact that in a system so complex, and involving so many factors, there must constantly arise emergencies requiring original thought, inventive adaptation of means to ends, and corresponding co-operative action on the part of numerous individuals, each with a separate duty assigned to him; all of which, humanly speaking, presupposes consultation, an interchange of ideas, and an agreement as to the part which each is to perform in the adaptation of means to ends; and this, in turn, presupposes a commensurate means of communication. It seems obvious, to start with, that no conceivable code of mere physical signals or sign language can possibly be adequate to the purpose, especially since the exchange of one or two strokes of their antennæ is sufficient to organize an army and promulgate a plan of campaign. It seems equally obvious that the only alternative hypothesis is that of thought-transference, rapport being established by physical contact in substantially the same way that it is established between unicellular organisms.

Unfortunately for our purpose, scientists have never studied the habits of ants with this hypothesis in view; and consequently the facts upon which we must rely are incidentally stated in connection with other matters. This, however, is not without its advantages from an evidential point of view. Romanes seems to have purposely avoided the question, and confines himself to the task of proving, through the writings of others (for example, Sir John Lubbock), that ants have a means of communication, but that it is not through the sense of hearing. He accuses Huber of dealing merely in " general statements as to ' contact of antennæ ' without narrating any particulars of his observations " (pp. 49 et seq.). The " Encyclopædia Britannica " (art. " Ant "), on the other hand, states that Huber took great interest in the question. and so strongly was he impressed by the fact of communion by antennæ " that he applied the term *langage antennal* " to the intercourse. Be this as it may in regard to his interest in ants, he certainly made some very striking experiments with bees on the same lines. Quoting from Büchner, Romanes prints the following : —

" Huber tested this communication by the antennæ by a striking experiment. He divided a hive into two separate parts by a partition wall, whereupon great excitement arose in the division in which there was no queen, and this was only quieted when some workers began to build royal cells. He then divided a hive in similar fashion by a trellis, through which bees could pass their feelers. In this case all remained quiet, and no attempt was made to build royal cells : the queen could also be clearly seen *crossing her antennæ with the workers* on the other side of the trellis."[1] (The italics are mine.)

Romanes also quotes De Fravière to show that bees " communicate information " by means of sounds, as follows: —

" As soon as a bee arrives with important news, it is at once surrounded, emits two or three shrill notes, and taps a comrade with its long, flexible, and very slender feelers, or antennæ. The friend passes the news in similar fashion, and the intelligence soon traverses the whole hive. If it is of an agreeable kind — if, for instance, it concerns the discovery of a store of sugar or of honey, or of a flowering meadow — all remains orderly. But, on the other hand, great excitement arises if the news presages some threatened danger, or if some strange animals are threatening invasion of the hive."

It thus appears that, Romanes to the contrary notwithstanding, the " shrill notes " uttered by the news-laden bee bear the same relation to the " communication of information " that the sound of a church-going bell bears to preaching. This, however, is a matter of minor importance in this discussion, for it is now well settled that whatever of specific information an ant or a bee desires to communicate to his fellows is transmitted, primarily, by means of physical contact in the manner stated. This is necessarily true of the ant; for, as I have already pointed out, no other sense is available for the purpose than the sense of touch or feeling. It is also a matter of doubt whether the bee is any better provided with the sense of hearing; for, as Romanes tells us, —

[1] Op. cit., p. 159.

17

" As in ants, so in bees. Sir John Lubbock's experiments failed to yield any evidence of a sense of hearing. But in this connection we must not forget the well-known fact, first observed by Huber, that the queen bee will answer by a certain sound. the peculiar piping of a pupa queen; and again, by making a certain cry or humming noise, will strike consternation suddenly on all the bees in the hive, — these remaining for a long time motionless as if stupefied." [1]

It seems probable, however, that the cry of queen answering to queen is merely an evidence of the fact that the queens are more highly endowed in this respect, as in many others, than the common bees; and the " humming " which strikes consternation on the whole hive is easily accounted for on the theory of physical vibrations transmitted from one to another. Besides, the paragraph quoted above, from De Fravière, fails to reveal any evidence whatever that the bees were affected in the least by the " shrill notes " of the bee bearing the portentous message. It was only after a general interchange of antennæ strokes that the excitement became visible.

Enough has now been said to establish the fact, provisionally, that specific information is conveyed by these insects to each other solely by means of physical contact, — touching each other with their antennæ. It remains to consider further the question whether the communication is made by means of a code of tactile signals, which has to be committed to memory by each individual. or by thought-transference, the antennal contact merely serving the purpose of establishing mental rapport between the commu-

[1] Op. cit., p. 144.

nicators. It is conceivable that a limited code of tactile signals might be in use which would serve the purposes of ordinary routine life; but when emergencies arise which no sagacity can foresee, and which present problems of which no experience can aid in the solution, the tactile-signal hypothesis falls of its weight.

I have space for but one illustrative incident. I select it, not because it is the best, for there are many recorded of a far more complicated nature, and involving more of co-operative action, but because it involves a situation that probably never was and never will be duplicated, and the antennal consultation was observed and recorded.

A gentleman's apiary was invaded by ants. In order to prevent future access the four legs of the beehive-stand were put into small shallow bowls filled with water. But owing to defective arrangements in other respects, the ants found their way into the hive several nights in succession. Finally, it was thought that all conditions were perfect.

" But once more the ants were found in the stand, and closer investigation showed that one of the bowls was dried up, and that a crowd of ants had gathered in it. But they found themselves puzzled how to go on with their robbery, for the leg did not, by chance, rest on the bottom of the bowl, but was about a half an inch from it. The ants were seen rapidly *touching each other with their antennæ*, or *carrying on a consultation*, until at last a rather larger ant came forward and put an end to the difficulty. It rose to its full height on its hind legs, and struggled until at last it seized a rather projecting splinter of the wooden leg, and managed to take hold of it. As soon as this was done other ants ran on to it, strengthened the hold by clinging, and so made a living bridge, over which the others could easily pass." [1]

It will thus be seen that the situation was unique, and the problem to be solved involved the co-operative action of several individuals, each with a distinct and separate duty to perform with intelligent reference to the general plan agreed upon at the antennal consultation. It may be objected that the essential thing was merely a case of bridge-building, which is common among ants. To this it is replied that all emergencies requiring the building of bridges by ants are necessarily unique, for each involves the solution of fresh engineering problems, the selection of suitable material from an unfamiliar vicinage, and the united action of hundreds of individuals, each performing the part assigned to him at the antennal consultation.

I submit that no conceivable code of mere tactile signals can possibly be equal to such an emergency. We must, therefore, seek a solution of the problem in some mental power or faculty, known to exist elsewhere, which is potentially equal to the task, provided it exists in the ant. In offering the hypothesis of thought-transference as a solution, I am not going outside of the region of known mental powers, nor of legitimate deductions therefrom. For I shall show, in the ensuing chapter, that thought-transference between human beings, under conditions of personal contact, is a very common phenomenon; and I shall claim the logical right to deduce from that fact my conclusions relating to the ant, on the ground that mind in that insect is the biological analogue of

---

[1] Op. cit., pp. 136, 137

mind in man. Having the same origin, they are governed by the same laws of progressive development; and if one, at a certain stage of mental evolution, develops the faculty of thought-transference, it follows that the other may do the same at the equivalent stage of mental development. And this is but another exemplification of the verity of the axiom of evolutionary science, that " the potentialities of manhood reside in the lowest unicellular organism."

CHAPTER VIII

THOUGHT–TRANSFERENCE BY MAN UNDER CONDITIONS OF PHYSICAL CONTACT

The Distinction between Thought-Transference and Telepathy. — The "Willing" Game. — The Muscle-Reading Hypothesis. — Instances of Thought-Transference which it does not explain. — Thought-Transference facilitated by Physical Contact. — The Spiritistic "Circle." — Experiments in Thought-Transference with and without Physical Contact — The Nervous Organism of Man specially adapted for Thought-Transference, and hence for Healing by Physical Contact.

BEFORE proceeding to discuss the subject of thought-transference by human beings under conditions of physical contact, I wish to say a word in regard to terminology, especially in reference to the distinction that should be observed between the terms " thought-transference " and " telepathy." The Century Dictionary treats them as synonyms, and much confusion in the popular mind has resulted. I do not hope, however, to reform this habit in the public mind. I merely wish to say that I shall use the word " telepathy " strictly as it has been defined by the Society for Psychical Research, — namely, to " cover all cases of impression received *at a distance* without the normal operation of the recognized sense organs." " Thought-transference," on the other hand, will be used to cover such cases of transferred mental impressions as occur at a not appreciable distance, — as when the agent and the percipient are in personal contact, or within touching distance; for example, when passes are made in close proximity to the person of the percipient or subject. The terms "agent" and "percipient" are applied in both telepathy and thought-transference, — the former to the one who sends the message, and the latter to the one who receives it.

As before stated, when the old mesmeric methods were employed, there was constant, or practically constant, contact between the operator and his subject. The result was that the higher phenomena — for example, thought-transference — were as constantly produced. It attracted the attention of the so-called "scientists" of the day, however, only to be met by wholesale denial and ridicule; and nothing worthy of the name was done by the latter to test the verity of the phenomena. Then, when the method of hypnotism, or Braidism, was found to be a labor-saving process of inducing the sleep, it was largely adopted by mesmerists, the result of which was that the higher phenomena were rarely produced; and in due time thought-transference was relegated, in the public mind, to the domain of exploded humbugs, or, at best, the lost arts, and "science" gained a temporary triumph.

In the meantime, however, some one invented what is familiarly known as the "willing game." There was no claim that there was any mesmerism, hypnotism, or magnetism in it; and so marvellous were some of the results that science consented to become interested in it, notwithstanding the claim that it demonstrated thought-transference. Dr. W. B. Carpenter, of London, was, I believe, the first to go on record with a description of the phenomena and a so-called scientific explanation. His description follows : —

" Several persons being assembled, one of them leaves the room, and during his absence some object is hidden. On the absentee's re-entrance, two persons who know the hiding-place stand, one on either side of him, and establish some personal contact with him, one method being to place one finger on the shoulder, while another is for each to place a hand on his body. He walks about the room between the two ' willers,' and generally succeeds before long in finding the hidden object, being led towards it, as careful observation and experiment have fully proved, by the involuntary muscular action of his unconscious guides, one or the other of them pressing more heavily when the object is on his side, and the finder as involuntarily turning toward that side." [1]

This conclusion was arrived at after a few experiments conducted in such a way as to exclude the possibility of disproving Dr. Carpenter's theory as to his particular experiments, or any other experiments conducted as he states above. There is, indeed, no possible doubt that experiments of that particular kind, and conducted in that particular way, are easily explicable under his hypothesis; for, as Dr. T. A. McGraw, of Detroit, later pointed out, it is practically impossible for human nature to resist the temptation to assist (consciously or unconsciously) in

[1] This quotation is found in the Proceedings of the Society for Psychical Research, vol. i p. 18. It is from Carpenter's " Mesmerism, Spiritualism, etc.," p. 54.

making the experiment a success. This is especially true of parlor entertainments conducted for the mere amusement of the spectators.

Be that as it may, Professor Carpenter labelled his explanation " muscle-reading," and muscle-reading it is to this day among those so-called scientists who seek to elevate their ignorance to the dignity of skepticism as to the verity of thought-transference or telepathy. Wherever personal contact is not excluded, every possible phase of thought-transference is dismissed with the one phrase " muscle-reading "! and all other phases of the phenomena are systematically denied. Thus, if a psychic correctly names every card in a pack, one after another in rapid succession, it is " muscle-reading " if she holds the hand of the agent; if not, it is trickery and legerdemain. If Mrs. Piper holds the hand of her sitter while she correctly relates the incidents of his past life, and tells correctly the names and ages of his family or friends, living or dead, it is " muscle-reading." If she performs the same feat without physical contact with the sitter, it is fraud and collusion. This, with all its monumental absurdity, expressed and implied, is the present attitude of so-called science — or rather, let us say, of some so-called scientists — with reference to thought-transference and telepathy.

Let us see what it implies. As the great Dr. Carpenter set the pace for that class of scientists, let us re-examine his words and compare them with the conclusions drawn by his followers. It will be observed that he carefully confines himself to one class of cases, namely, those wherein the psychic is required to do something, — for example, walk about the room in search of a hidden object. The "willers" place their hands upon his shoulders and accompany him about the room, strongly "willing" him to find the hidden object. Dr. Carpenter infers that the psychic was led to it "by the involuntary muscular action of his unconscious guides, one or the other of them pressing more heavily when the object is on his side, and the finder as involuntarily turning toward that side."

The theory, in other words, is that the psychic is pushed or pulled in the right direction by muscular action alone, voluntary or involuntary. And who will, or can, deny the justness of this conclusion drawn from the premises as stated by Dr. Carpenter? But does it justify the conclusion that "muscular action" can be pressed into service to enable a psychic (normal acquisition of knowledge being out of the question) to give correctly names of persons, dates of events, denominations of cards, or to relate an anecdote that is verifiable only by subsequent research? The question answers itself; and yet all this is included in the "muscle-reading" hypothesis of the so-called science of the day.

The Society for Psychical Research felt compelled to pay attention to the hypothesis for the purpose of showing that, whilst Dr. Carpenter's conclusions might be justified in the limited field which he explored, it could not be pressed beyond its boundaries. To that end its committee cited numerous instances, in contact cases, that were clearly inexplicable on the theory of muscle-reading. But the efforts of the committee were chiefly directed toward proving that the same things could be done without personal contact. In this, as all the world knows, — except the class of "scientists" named, — they succeeded so far as to demonstrate telepathy beyond a peradventure. Unfortunately for my present purpose I am not in a position to avail myself of their labors. It would be a work of supererogation, at this late day, to undertake to demonstrate to readers of this book the verity of telepathy as a faculty of the human mind. Telepathy will, therefore, be taken for granted.

What I wish to show is that thought-transference is greatly facilitated by personal contact; and as the labors of the Society for Psychical Research were not directed to that object, the illustrative incidents are not so plentiful as could be desired. Nevertheless, I hope to make up for it by appealing to the experience of every one who has taken an intelligent interest in psychical research.

I will cite one case, however, which will serve to illustrate my meaning. It is found on page 55 of Vol. I. of the Proceedings of the Society. It is stated as follows : —

" My daughter, who had recently returned from a visit to her brother at his vicarage, asked M. B. (who was again seated with eyes bandaged and pencil in hand), 'Who preached at my brother's church last Sunday evening?' the answer to the question being known to my daughter *only*. M. B. wrote the first six letters of the name, viz., 'Westmo—,' and then said, 'I feel no more influence.' My daughter said, 'Lean your head against me.' M. B. did so, and then wrote the rest of the name, making it quite right — 'Westmore.' "

It is clear that Dr. Carpenter would not have regarded the first part of this answer as coming within his "muscle-reading" hypothesis, for there was no contact whatever; and it would require the united efforts of a large number of his most devoted followers to believe that a momentary contact of the head of the psychic with the clothing of the "willer" would enable her to complete the word by "muscle-reading." as Dr. Carpenter defined it. In other words, it would require a large amount of "scientific credulity" to believe that this momentary contact could convey from one to the other the remaining letters of the name. by "unconscious muscular action on the part of one person, and automatically interpreted by the other."

In strict justice, however, to those scientists who find a universal solvent for all contact cases in "muscle-reading," it must be stated that the above-named Society set the pace at the beginning of its labors by agreeing to relegate indiscriminately all contact cases to the domain of muscle-reading. It is needless to say that adherence to this rule has led the Society and its followers into innumerable absurdities, and greatly retarded its own progress in the investigation of some important phases of psychic phenomena, — for example, mesmerism. It was a tub thrown to the scientific whale; albeit it will yet be found that the tub. thus recklessly thrown away. was one of its most valuable assets For if it is true that thought-transference is facilitated to an appreciable extent by psychical contact between agent and percipient, it is a fact in nature that science cannot safely ignore. Necessarily such a fact is invested with profound significance; and the Society for Psychical Research, when it assumed to ignore it in deference to an insensate prejudice born of profound ignorance, wronged itself and indefinitely retarded the progress of the investigation it was organized to prosecute. It is an axiom of science that no fact or phenomenon, however insignificant it may seem to be, can safely be disregarded in an inductive investigation of the problems of nature; for it often happens that a phenomenon which in itself is apparently destitute of scientific significance furnishes a solvent for the most important problems when considered in its relations to other phenomena.

It would not be difficult to show that the Society has seriously handicapped itself by ignoring phenomena that afford a complete and valid explanation of many important psychological problems. That, however, is a question of no practical importance to us in this inquiry, although the points wherein it failed will appear incidentally as we proceed. The question with which we are now concerned is, Does physical contact between agent and percipient facilitate thought-transference? In presenting the evidence on this point I can safely appeal to the observation and experience of thousands who have come in contact with so-called spirit mediums. Any one who has attended an old-fashioned spiritistic seance will recall the fact that physical contact between members of the circle was considered an essential prerequisite to success in obtaining phenomena. Usually the whole company, including the medium, were seated around the table, each member of the circle clasping the hand of his neighbor on either side. Various reasons were given for this practice. but, whatever the reason assigned, each medium considered it an essential condition of success. Hence they were designated as "circles"; and each member was strictly enjoined not to break the continuity of the circle. The fact that this condition was, for some reason, essential to success was demonstrated by the phenomena; thus, as long as the circle remained unbroken, a good medium would have at her command the thoughts of all present, but the moment that the contact was broken anywhere in the circle the medium would immediately become aware of the fact and complain of "inharmonious conditions." Many mediums were able to locate the exact point where contact was broken; others could locate a skeptic anywhere in the circle; and some would be unable to proceed until the offending member was ousted from the circle.

Spiritists, of course, will say that these phenomena had nothing whatever to do with thought-transference between living persons, and that it was all due to the limitations of spiritual intercourse. This question need not be argued in this connection, for such phenomena do not stand alone as evidence of the point we wish to make. The same phenomena occur in experimental thought-transference where physical conditions are the same. That is to say, thought-transference is almost invariably facilitated by physical contact between the agent and the percipient. I have made hundreds of experiments with the view of testing this question, while at the same time eliminating the possible element of muscle-reading. Thus, I assume that when a telepathist, under test conditions, correctly states the denomination of a card drawn at random from a pack, there is no possible code of signals, consciously or unconsciously employed, that will enable one person to convey to another a statement that the jack of clubs has been drawn from the pack. And when nine-tenths of all the cards in the pack are correctly named in rapid succession, it is safe to assume that "muscle-reading," in the sense in which Dr. Carpenter employed it, is ridiculously inadequate to explain the phenomena. I have repeatedly made the following experiment: Selecting a company of six or eight persons, I would securely blindfold one of the party to act as the percipient, then draw a card at random from a pack and place it on a table in full view of every one, except of course the percipient. Under such circumstances telepathy is comparatively easy, provided the members of the company are earnest and harmonious; but I have invariably noted that where the percipient is new to the experiment his lucidity is greatly promoted by forming a circle of which he is a part. It is an exceptionally good psychic who can dispense with physical contact in the beginning of his career. The same remarks apply to phenomena other than card-reading.

I once had the privilege of experimenting with one of the best telepathists in the United States. She could read in rapid succession a whole pack of cards without an error. During the course of my experiments I was induced to commit the unpardonable folly of trying to convince a so-called scientist of the fact that telepathy was a power of the human mind. In making the experiment I caused him to purchase a new pack of cards from a neighboring store, to shuffle them himself behind the back of the psychic, who was also blindfolded to the entire satisfaction of the scientist. In pursuance of instructions, he drew a card from the centre of the pack and exhibited it to me. The lady was somewhat embarrassed at first and hesitated somewhat in naming the card; finally she asked me to take hold of her hand, whereupon she instantly named the card. This was repeated in rapid succession until the whole pack was exhausted. This feat having been performed without an error, the scientist was asked to express an opinion. This he did with great promptitude and alacrity by informing me that it was all " muscle-reading." Neither myself nor the psychic had anticipated such a reply under the circumstances, whereupon she offered to repeat the experiment without physical contact. The challenge was accepted and the scientist was allowed to prescribe his own conditions. The result was that the lady named more than half of the cards correctly. The falling off was doubtless due to embarrassment and over-anxiety, and partly to the fact that thought-transference is facilitated by physical contact.

It should be remarked in this connection that these experiments were not made with special reference to testing the question of thought-transference by physical contact. I could, however, fill many volumes the size of this with incidents demonstrative of the proposition that physical contact does facilitate thought-transference in cases where muscle-reading is simply out of the question. It remains to inquire what is the physical mechanism that enables this to be done. The answer is not far to seek, and the reader has already anticipated me, when I say that the nervous organism of man appears to be specially designed for that purpose. Everybody knows that the nerves have their terminals in the cuticle; that the terminal nerve cells are more highly differentiated than almost any others, especially those located in the tips of the fingers. They are differentiated with special reference to the conveyance and reception of intelligence. The result is that when contact is made with another by the laying on of hands, a chain of communication is established between the subjective minds of the two individuals. It follows that physical contact by laying on of hands brings each and every cell of the bodies of both the agent and the percipient into potential rapport, and that this rapport may be made actual by a proper mental effort.

It will now be seen that man is endowed with the requisite mechanism for mental healing by means of physical contact.

18

CHAPTER IX

CONCLUSIONS — THEORETICAL AND PRACTICAL

The Hypothetical Magnetic Fluid. — Histionic Suggestion competent to explain all the Facts of Mesmerism. — This Form of Suggestion the most effective as a Therapeutic Agency. — It may operate independently of the Volition of the Patient. — The Nerve Terminals the Means provided by Nature for the Transmission of Histionic Suggestions. — The Spinal Column the Guide to one Set of Terminals, and Pain the Guide to the other. — This Process of Treatment available to all.

HAVING now definitely ascertained the existence of a law of mental medicine hitherto unrecognized, it remains to inquire what conclusions, practical and theoretical, are derivable therefrom. The first conclusion is in reference to its bearing upon the question of mesmerism. It is obvious at a glance that the old theory of fluidic emanations, or animal magnetism, so called, is, to say the least, unnecessary. And it is an axiom of science that an unnecessary theory is necessarily wrong.

The theory of fluidic emanations has held its place in the minds of a large number of people simply for the want of a rational hypothesis that would otherwise explain the phenomena; and this, notwithstanding the fact that it accounts for but a very small portion of them, and fails entirely in the most vital and essential particulars. Thus, the fact that concentration of mind on the part of the healer is essential to success reveals the fact that the process of healing is a purely mental one, and is not due to a fluidic emanation from the healer in the nature of magnetism. In fact, Deleuze, the ablest of the old writers on the subject of mesmerism, and an advocate of the magnetic theory, admitted that the existence of the hypothetical magnetic fluid was far from being demonstrated. Nor did he seem to regard it as possible to demonstrate its existence. On the contrary, in his work on " Instruction in Animal Magnetism " (Hartshorn's translation), he begins by laying down thirty-four " general principles " of animal magnetism, upwards of twenty of which exclude the magnetic theory. That is to say, the great bulk of his general principles presupposed a definite mental condition, and prescribed a specific mental attitude, on the part of the healer, as prerequisites to successful work. It is needless to say that these are conditions as far removed as possible from those which one would naturally suppose to be requisite under the theory of fluidic emanations. To say the least, both theories are unnecessary. Both theories, therefore, under the law of parsimony, cannot be true. We must, therefore, make a choice between the theory of fluidic emanations, or animal magnetism, and that of the transmission of intelligence by means of physical contact, or histionic suggestion, — provided, of course, that one of the hypotheses is competent to explain all the facts. Otherwise both must be rejected.

Without stopping to argue the question further, I assume that I have already shown that the hypothesis of histionic suggestion is clearly competent to explain all the facts of mesmerism, and remove all that is mysterious in its phenomena from the domains of mysticism and superstition. If it is capable of this task, it follows that all cognate phenomena are explicable under the same hypothesis; and these comprise a vast congeries of the most important psychic phenomena that have puzzled man and filled him with superstitious dread throughout all the ages.

It would be a work of supererogation to attempt to classify all the various phases of these phenomena. The intelligent reader has already done so for himself, as the application of the principles is perfectly obvious. I cannot refrain, however, from remarking upon the subject in its relations to mental medicine. The first thing to be observed is that this law does not conflict with the psychological aspects of mental medicine as developed in Part I. of this book. That is to say, the Law of Suggestion is the dominant energy which controls therapeutic action in all cases. Histionic suggestion is merely another form of suggestion, and it is, I venture to assert, the most effective of all methods or forms of that agency.

From a historical point of view the theory of histionic suggestion is invested with transcendent interest and importance. The wonderful cures effected through all the ages by the laying on of hands has hitherto found no scientific explanation beyond that afforded by the theory of oral suggestion. The same may be said of the phenomena produced by mesmeric processes. It is now seen, however, that a potent energy is released by physical contact, and made available for healing the sick. It is the most potent form of suggestion known, for the reason that it may operate independently of the volition of the patient. This would seem, at first glance, to form an exception to the rule that the faith of the patient is always essential to success in mental healing. The fact is, however, that it is merely a question of degree. That is to say, the mental energy of the healer is transmitted directly or indirectly through the nerves to the seat of the disease; and the active co-operation of the subjective mind of the patient is not always essential, a state of passivity being all that is required. This is easily secured in therapeutical cases; for one is not prone to active opposition to the restoration of his health, even though his judgment may regard the means as of doubtful efficiency. It was this fact that enabled Jesus, in his native village, to heal the sick by the laying on of hands. although he failed to do many wonderful works in that city " because of their unbelief."

And this is why children too young to be affected by the ordinary forms of suggestion are peculiarly susceptible to mesmeric treatment or treatment by the laying on of hands. The old mesmerists, indeed, claimed to be able to heal domestic animals by mesmeric passes or by the laying on of hands. It was upon this assertion that one of their strongest arguments for the magnetic theory was built. " It could not be a mental impression," they urged, " because neither animals nor young children were able to understand the import of a mental suggestion." But this argument falls to the ground in view of the well-ascertained fact that emotional and therapeutic impulses can be conveyed by thought-transference in cases where it is impossible to transmit an intelligible message involving the use of words. The Society for Psychical Research, in the course of their investigations. established this fact beyond a doubt: and Ochorowicz, in his monumental work on Mental Suggestion, has demonstrated the same proposition.

It will thus be seen that histionic suggestion is by far the most powerful of all the forms in which that agency can be employed, because it is the most direct and most positive.

The question remains. What facilities has nature provided for the transmission of histionic suggestions? The success which the laying on of hands has met with in all the ages would seem to indicate that the exact process of healing by those methods is a matter of indifference; that is to say, it would seem that physical contact with almost any part of the body would be effective. To a certain extent this is undoubtedly true. That is to say. contact with any nerve in the body places the operator in communication, directly or indirectly, with every other nerve in the body; and therapeutic impulses may therefore be conveyed from any point of contact. Nevertheless, there is always a right way and a wrong way of doing anything. It is obvious that the best way to convey a therapeutic impulse to an affected part of the body is to follow the lines of least resistance: these lines are undoubtedly those that reach the affected part most directly. It follows that some knowledge of anatomy is very useful to the operator in determining the best method of procedure. Fortunately. however, nature has provided a means by which any one may obtain a practical knowledge sufficient to enable him to practise histionic suggestion in the most effective manner. A few words will make my meaning clear.

Obviously the most effective method of reaching a diseased part is the most direct method; that is to say, given a diseased organ, the terminals of the nerves which reach that organ are the ones to be treated.

Again, we are assisted in reaching a definite conclusion by the researches of modern medical science; and again a tribute of admiration is extorted for the manner in which nature has provided the means by which practice under this system is rendered available to all. Turning to the great work of Dr. John Hilton, an eminent English physician, entitled " Rest and Pain; or, The Therapeutic Influence of Rest and the Diagnostic Value of Pain," we find that nature has provided a means by which the humblest cell in the human body can be reached with absolute certainty.

Dr. Hilton points out that there are two ways of reaching each individual organ of the human body through the nervous system: that is to say, there are two nerve terminals available for treatment by the laying on of hands. One system lies along each side of the spinal column, the nerves projecting to the surface " from the vertebral canal through the intervertebral foramina, close to the bones or the intervertebral substances."

It is safe to say that, by digital manipulation of these nerve terminals, any organ of the human body may be reached directly. If the operator possesses a sufficient knowledge of the nervous system, he may of course save a little time and labor by selecting the

right nerve at once. This, however, is unnecessary
from a practical point of view, for the reason that the
whole spinal column can be manipulated with but
little extra trouble; and the beneficial effect of a
treatment of the whole spinal column amply compen-
sates for all the labor expended. Besides, it often
happens that more than one organ is affected sympa-
thetically, and requires treatment accordingly. Dr.
Hilton also shows that each organ, each muscle, and
each joint of the body furnish also a distribution of
the nerves to the skin over the insertions of the same
muscles. It is to this fact that the doctor alludes
when he speaks of the diagnostic value of pain. It
will thus be seen that nature has provided a sure guide
to the peripheral nerve terminals of every organ of
the human body. The doctor points out that in some
cases the seat of the disease when in the muscles or
joints may be somewhat remote from the nerve terminals where the pain is manifested. The treatment,
however, whatever it may be, must be made where
the pain manifests itself. It is needless to say that
Dr. Hilton makes no mention of other than the or-
thodox treatment of the old school of medicine. The
applicability of his facts, however, to treatment by the
laying on of hands is self-evident. All there is to do
is to manipulate or massage one or both of the two
sets of nerve terminals. The spinal column is the
guide to one set of terminals, and pain the guide to
the other.

The question will now be asked, Is this process of
treatment available to all alike? My answer is, No!
That is to say, there are different degrees of efficiency
in different individuals; the highest degree being

attainable by well-developed psychics. The treatment, however, is available to all in a greater or less degree; and practice will enable any one in a short time to attain a high degree of efficiency. The essential thing to be observed in all cases is that the mind must be concentrated upon the work in hand: otherwise the work is purely mechanical, depending for its efficiency upon mechanical stimulation of the nerves, the same as in ordinary massage. It is, however, more efficient than ordinary massage, because the effect is more direct upon the nerves involved. It is, indeed, in all its phases nature's remedy for disease, and it is instinctively employed in thousands of instances; for example, when the sympathetic mother soothes her nervous and restless infant by rubbing her hand on its bare back.

It will thus be seen that the process is simple to the last degree, and requires no further elucidation to enable any intelligent person to put it into immediate and effective practice.

THE END

CPSIA information can be obtained
at www.ICGtesting.com
Printed in the USA
BVHW020009100223
658265BV00031B/627